Dedicated to all cognitively virtuous citizens.

Thank you for adopting an attitude toward thinking that:
supports a healthy self-image
builds confidence
grows acceptance and trustworthiness
evokes gratitude
and is based on joy.

CONTENTS

I Don't Trust Myself
to Make Decisions

Charlie: (friendly Go Daddy customer service rep) I see, Ms. Novak, that you have several domain names and sites. Wait, it looks like you have some on a couple different accounts. Okay, let's see here, we've got conceptbridges.com, terrienovak.com, a hypothesis site, decision-doctor.com, decisiond-o-u-l-a.com? What do you do?

Me: (the name and title indecision obvious and feeling a bit of irony coming on in 3, 2, 1 . . .) I help people make decisions. It's decision doula—where a doula is a birthing coach. I help people birth decisions. That's what I do: help people make decisions that bring about change.

Charlie: (with a smile in his voice, obviously enjoying the people part of his job) What advice do you have for me? I'm terrible at making decisions. I could really use your advice; I could use the advice you give others.

Me: (pondering how cool a website support job is—learning from experts and business owners every day) What do you do now to make decisions?

Charlie: (without hesitation) I ask all my friends what they would do. Because I totally don't trust myself. So I go to the people I *do* trust and I tell them what I am trying to decide. And boy, I am really surprised a lot of times what they think, it's nothing like what I was thinking of doing. Actually, *most* the time it's nothing like what I was thinking of doing. I am so glad I asked their opinions, because otherwise I would be totally screwed. I am fine with little day-to-day decisions, but when it comes to something really big and important, I ask my friends.

Me: (impressed he recognizes he has a decision process) That sounds like a tried and true plan. I admire that you are reaching out to people. You must really trust your friends, and you're able to communicate what you need; but Charlie, it sounds like there's a really important person you're forgetting to ask.

Charlie: (showing genuine interest) Oh? who's that?

Me: (Okay Terrie, here's your four seconds of influence) Well, yourself. You need to give yourself permission to reach inside and understand how you are feeling about the topic and let *yourself* weigh in, along with the information from your friends. You know all the factors in the situation better than anyone. You will need to feel good about the decision in order to do what it takes to move forward.

Charlie: (demonstrating change ain't easy) I don't know if I can do that. I just . . . I don't trust myself.

Me: Well, that's what we're all here for, isn't it? Encouraging each other to have confidence? To show each other how to build self-trust so that we can make decisions we and those around us can live with? That's what supporting each other really is. Right? You help people make decisions every day, don't you?

Charlie: (with a sigh) Yeah, sure. I guess I do.

Me: Well, you are helping me right now. You're recommending I decide to put all domains under one account, right? I trust your expertise and my gut is telling me that seems like the exact right thing to do. Let's go ahead and do what it takes to make that change happen.

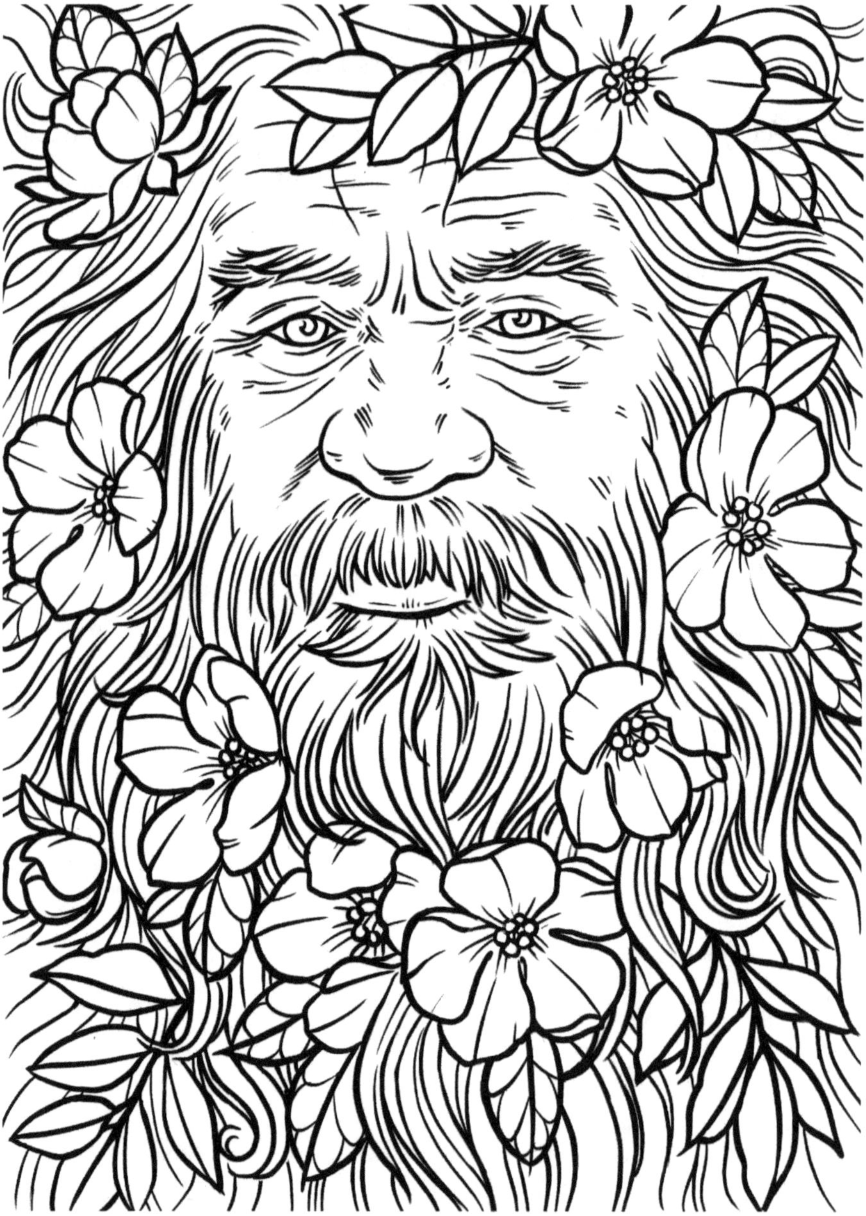

CHAPTER · 1

WHAT SCHOOL NEVER TAUGHT
YOU ABOUT CRITICAL THINKING

I'm a business systems analyst, and I am going to talk about the system of decision making.

Here's a quick definition just to get us going.

> **System:**
> a set of procedures used to get something done.

How do you explain it when people around you are making decisions in a way that seems completely off the wall? They decide, and others are left to run around and clean up after them. Aren't they *doing it wrong*?

Or better yet: how do you explain it when people make a decision using their gut feelings to put a hunch into action, and it ends up a wild success? It's unclear how a successful result could even be possible, yet it is. Are *they doing it right*?

Take, for example, Amazon Prime. I mention Amazon because it's very relatable for people. I had a colleague who was working in Portland, Oregon, and she was preparing to move her family back to their home in New Zealand. I asked her what she was going to miss most about living in the U.S. and she said, "To be honest, I'm really going to miss Amazon Prime."

How did free fast shipping come to the top of the list of things to love in America? I'm sure it has something to do with undeniable guilty pleasure of receiving a box to open at your doorstep, and Jeff Bezos, founder and CEO of Amazon.com, tells us the decision to greenlight Amazon Prime was ultimately based on intuition.[1]

"There wasn't a single financially savvy person who supported the decision to launch Amazon Prime. Zero. Every spreadsheet showed that it was going to be a disaster," said Bezos. "So that had to just be made with gut. Those kinds of decisions, they cannot be made analytically, so far as I know. They have to be made with gut."

I found myself asking, just how does one make a decision 'with gut'?

I have a degree in physics and went on to make a career in software engineering. I spent most of my professional life facilitating other people's decisions so engineering teams could get product out to market. As my career matured I wore many hats: coder, project manager; then I found my strength as a systems analyst. Throughout this journey I followed the typical professional development avenues and acquired several industry-standard, best-practice certifications.

Every day we hear about the use of intuition by innovative organizations and individuals, like in the case of Amazon Prime. Heck, Bezos pretty much brags about the fact that it was his intuition that brought this new business model forward.

Yet somehow, nowhere in the best-practices certifications I invested in over the years was a methodology of how to integrate intuition into the multitude of decisions necessary to deliver a product to market. Why is it that despite the potential value in intuition, the industry training machine seems to value rational thinking, and to completely disregard intuition? Is that only written in the CEO training material? Did I sleep through that chapter? What was I missing?

I pulled up the e-version of the certification-worthy Business Analysis Body of Knowledge (BABOK)[2] developed and promoted by the International Institute of Business Analysis, and I did a few word searches. The word *decision* is mentioned a whopping 462 times. Honestly, this was no surprise to me; the ability to facilitate decisions is acknowledged as an 'underlying competency' for analysts and techniques in the system of decision making are found in every chapter. However, the words *gut* and *hunch* appear zero times in the text. Still not surprised; the IIBA is too nerdy to use those words anyway. The word *intuition* is mentioned *once* in this context: "analyst needs to rely on intuition in the conceptual thought process." That's it.

The BABOK is a comprehensive 514-page document that describes the "practice of enabling change in an enterprise by defining needs and recommending solutions that deliver value." This is the text I was trained and certified in, and had my own professional performance rated against.

Yet how to apply the highly revered quality of intuition in decision making is completely missing.

As a professional who's well paid and trained on the company dollar to provide recommendations to decision makers, I essentially had intuition trained right out of me.

Why is that? Why is intuition seen as sloppy and inaccurate even though it is commonly known to be widely used in business? And in science, for that matter.

It's well understood that groundbreaking scientific research may start with intuitive knowledge that leads to the development of hypotheses, which can later be validated through testing and analysis. This scientific research approach describes exactly how I (finally) stumbled into recognizing the importance of intuition in decision making.

For me, my rediscovery of the power of my intuition went like this: I'm fifty years old, and my doctor delivers a diagnosis of stage zero cervical cancer (HPV and cervical lesions). He clearly states I am too old to naturally regress (like 90% of younger women do), and prescribes a treatment to surgically remove half my cervix.

Yet I had a 'gut feeling' that removing a body part at that time just didn't seem right. There was no cancer, yet there were no treatment options offered. To jump to surgery gave me the feeling I was being 'underserved' as a woman. I choose to *not* set up the surgery appointment and to find another way.

I could hardly believe this was me. I took actions based on my gut and not from the advice of an expert professional? How unscientific of me! I wasn't following the rules. Was I scared or just crazy?

After some investigation, I found the only other treatment options available were those considered to be *alternative* medicine. As a complete skeptic, I decided to follow my intuition and allow time for my body to regress naturally. Meanwhile, I began a healing experiment on my own body based on treatments offered by a reputable naturopath and my trusted yoga teacher. I committed to boosting my immune system with a non-inflammatory diet, supplements and natural topical treatments. I began meditation techniques including chanting, breathing and body exercises. I carefully followed the alternative treatments as prescribed and monitored progress with regular HPV and cervical cell screenings. The lab results showed the abnormal cells declined until finally, almost three years later, there was a full regression to normal cells and no active HPV infection.

A completely successful regression based on decisions that were the absolute opposite of my doctor's recommendation and *based solely on my gut feeling.*

Was this an example of decision-making luck? Or is there something else at play here?

It is time to stop the witch hunt on intuition and see it for what it is: a fast, automatic, subconscious processing style that can provide us with very useful information that deliberate analyzing can't. We need to accept that intuitive and analytic thinking should occur together, and be weighed up against each other in difficult decision-making situations.

Dr. Valerie van Mulukom, neuroscientist

A PROCESS THAT ENABLES THE POWER OF BOTH THINKING AND FEELING

Every person or organization who has put effort into making a change knows there is a process they need to follow.

This process involves a series of decisions. Decisions, and the actions that result from decisions, move them forward in the project plan. All along the way there is frequent progress monitoring and communication with everyone involved. Leaders know from experience that change is hard and scary to people who are even on the very fringe of being affected. Why is it that people so consistently feel this fear of change?

On reason might be that somewhere deep down inside, everyone knows that change is based on decisions, and the nature of decisions is that they are unpredictable and unproven. If it was predictable and proven, there wouldn't need to be any decisions, it would just be a checklist of things to do. Bottom line, we just *know* that when decision making is needed, the results are a gamble.[3] As an analyst, I spend a fair amount of my time pinning down who is the decision maker, the one accountable for the gamble.

On the other hand, few people or organizations understand exactly what is needed to obtain the confidence necessary to stay motivated to do all the work, all that scary work, that is directed by that gamble of a decision. Often times activities are worked into projects to gain or sustain 'momentum,' like mini-celebrations at milestones or team-building exercises. Maybe even comfort items are introduced to a project team, like free food. These things seem to refresh energy, but it's hard to say if they *grow confidence* along the rocky path to implementing the desired change.

It's worth noting that, by *desired change*, I mean a transformation that can be fully embraced and continuously built upon. A desired result is one you are expecting, accountable for, and proud to own. How many projects get those kinds of results? There have been studies that say less than 30% of information technology projects bring about the expected results; so, confidence in getting what you expect is arguably on shaky ground.

When I was observing the series of decisions I made during my own HPV Healing Experiment, I made a discovery which profoundly changed my view on how I think people should be making decisions.

It turns out that the more complex and ambiguous the decision is, the more *essential* it becomes to include intuition in decision making.

> The more complex and ambiguous the decision is, the more *essential* it becomes to include intuition in decision making.

So, I created a process for bringing about change that weaves together analytical thinking and intuition.

It's a simple process that sits within a high-level framework that is essentially a simple, logical process.

WHAT DO A PROCESS AND AN EASY-BAKE OVEN HAVE IN COMMON?

I need to take a small step back and explain what a *process* involves.

> **Process (n.):**
> A process transforms an input into an output.

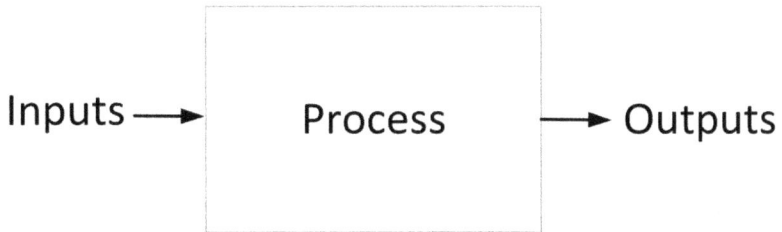

Inputs ⟶ Process ⟶ Outputs

When we consider the *process of decision making*, it looks like this.

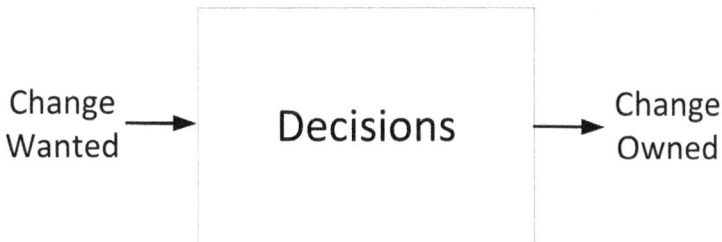

Change Wanted ⟶ Decisions ⟶ Change Owned

The input is the change you want; the process is all the decisions that get stuff done; the output is having and owning the actual change.

In my mind, I see a process like an Easy-Bake Oven.[4] Thank you Kenner, for brainwashing me with your slick advertising. Yes, go ahead and watch the vintage commercial in the endnote, you can see the transformation right before your eyes in 32 seconds. It goes like this: I really want cake, so I put batter into the oven. A lot of things happen in that oven. Some things are in my control, like what kind of light-bulb I put in the oven and how long the pan stays inside. Somethings are out of my control, like how heat changes the ingredients that start as goop into something chewy. I simply trust in that part, not fully understanding it, but completely counting on it! Then what comes out the other side of the oven is a cake. Frankly, it's kind of a magical transformation, with the result looking nothing like what went in. And that incredible freshly baked cake smell! The aroma created puts a smile on everyone's face. I have to let it cool, and even then, it's not quite ready. There is still some frosting and decorating to do, and all while fending off my brother!

Ok, so we have a good image about what a process is, and how it transforms in input to an output. But how is decision making a process?

Let's look carefully at an example most of us are familiar with:

Consider the decision to change your job.

Remember that job you chose to stay in too long?

During that time when you were thinking about a changing your job, who encouraged you to listen to your intuition or prioritize your joy? Probably no one did. You likely reviewed your current salary and benefits. You may have thought about how invested you were in having created many relationships within your current organization. You may have thought about all the time you invested becoming proficient in the tools your organization used in their operations. You may have heard on the news about a pending downturn in job market conditions and difficulties in hiring your unique skill set. Maybe you couldn't find the energy or time to proactively do all those things it takes to perform a job search. The thought of changing your commute, your schedule, your location, and more; it all seemed pretty overwhelming. You did make a decision, though—you went with the 'do-nothing' option, and you continued to make this decision for too long.

Now consider that time you chose to pursue a new job.

During that time, were you listening to your intuition? Did anyone encourage you to look into how you felt about your current conditions? Did you think about the things that really give you *joy* in a job? Maybe you made a list of your preferences, and even prioritized this list. Did you **accept** that it was time to leave your current job behind you and start visualizing how you would apply your unique skill set in a new environment that made you feel like a productive contributor? Did you feel grateful to those who made recommendations and referred you? All these things seemed to give you the energy and time to keep moving forward in the job search. Did you **thank** the people who took the interest in getting to know you and interview you? Maybe you even sent them a note. Did you **trust** the new company when you negotiated your new salary and benefits? Were you committed to making your new position *successful going forward?* You may have even asked in your interview questions about what would make you successful in the position, so you could assess if that fit your beliefs and values.

You see, this time, with your preferences clearly in mind, you had the motivation to do what it took to keep moving forward toward your goal.

It's clear that joy, acceptance, thankfulness and trust are *not* analytical, nor data informed. Yet those parts of your decision making were essential in executing a complicated decision in a high-quality fashion. In the decision to 'do nothing' elements were not even present. I offer this idea: we can consider joy, acceptance, thankfulness and trust as tangible expressions of *intuition*.

> Joy, acceptance, thankfulness and trust are expressions of intuition.

People who go with their gut are more passionate protectors of their choice.

Stephanie Pappas, neuroscience writer[5]

With the assistance of intuition, the energy and resources to go into *action* just seemed there for you. You committed to doing all those job-seeking activities, even though there were tough times of frustration and set-backs. You didn't stop because you just *knew* you could do this *all the way* until you got the result you expected—a new job.

> You made the choice to change using *both* thinking and feeling.

RECOGNIZING INTUITION

Merriam-Webster defines intuition as "quick and ready insight," but then goes on to further define it as "a power [seriously, *a power*] of attaining knowledge without evident rational thought."

A power of knowing without thinking? Yes please, more of that!

So I looked deeper, into Sanskrit, the mother of most of the living languages. There is a word, *buddhi*, that is defined as "the ability of the mind to know, judge, discriminate, and decide."

Yoga practitioners are encouraged to regularly practice and build their buddhi skills, then learn to apply it. The starting place in this practice is to observe how buddhi functions when a decision is made (just like we did in the job change process). In the decision-making process, buddhi is the clear calm inner wisdom, that can be described as the inner voice; it knows what is truly right for you at any given moment.

> **Intuition:**
> The clear, calm inner wisdom that knows what is truly right.

Basically, your intuition wants whatever you value most.

It's not only listening to but also *trusting* your intuition that enables you to take advantage of this wisdom. Many people, like myself, had intuition practically trained out of them throughout their lives. Somehow, we stopped practicing using it and stopped recognizing it when it presents itself. This leaves us at a disadvantage when it comes to innovative decision making. Time and time again, we see that the best business leaders and the most successful people listen to their intuition.

Have the courage to follow your heart and intuition. They somehow already know what you truly want to become.

Steve Jobs

DECIDING FROM THE INSIDE

Here's the process that describes what is involved when we include our inner wisdom when we make choices. It's the original decision-making process, now updated with elements of intuition overlaid. Key elements of intuition are represented by incorporating Joy, Acceptance, Trust, and Thankfulness in choice-making activities.

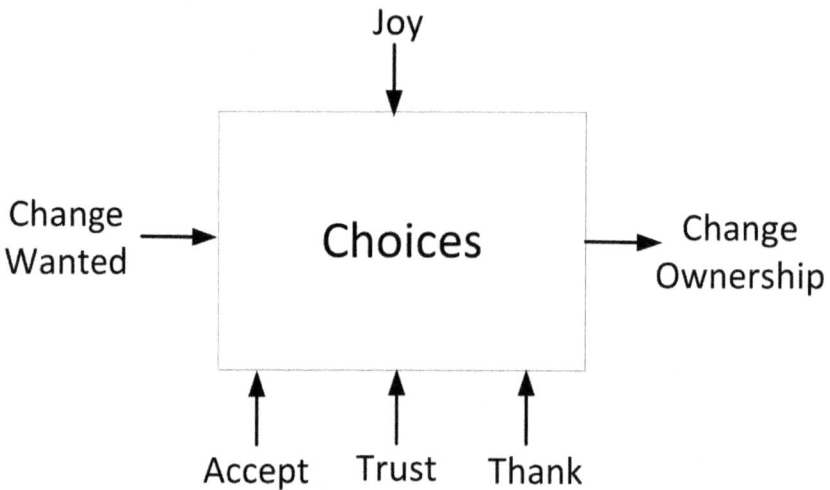

```
                    Joy
                     |
                     v
  Change    -->  ┌─────────┐  -->  Change
  Wanted         │ Choices │       Ownership
                 └─────────┘
                   ^    ^    ^
                   |    |    |
                Accept Trust Thank
```

Later, when we drill into the process a little deeper, I will share the three strategies to take us through all the choices needed to transform the desired change into the realized change, but for now, this model helps us see the influence our gut feeling is having on the desired outcome.

TWO GREAT TASTES THAT TASTE GREAT TOGETHER[6]

Science tells us we don't have to worry about our intuition degrading the quality of analysis involved in critical and rational thinking.

Nor do we have to worry that we are somehow short-changing our intuitive abilities by taking the time to do thoughtful analysis.

Over fifty years of research has converged on the importance of individual differences in use of intuition and analysis. When combining data from multiple studies of the relationship between intuition and analysis, the findings support the view that intuition and analysis are *independent* constructs.[7]

That means intuition and analysis can be used successfully, together, for the highest quality decisions.

> Use both analysis and intuition when your intent is to design and create change.

CRITICAL THINKING AND INTUITIVE THINKING

There is a lot of conversation recently in social media about the importance of critical thinking—and what happens when it's lacking. A popular belief has somehow come about that we are not good at critical thinking anymore; that not enough people are thinking critically, and our educational system is failing to teach students how to think critically.

According to Criticalthinking.org, the fundamental reason why so much school learning is not effectively transferred to real life is that it lacks the *intuitive basis*, the insights, for the translation.

So how do critical thinking and intuition intersect?

Critical thinking is the practice of objectively analyzing a situation by gathering information from all possible sources, and then evaluating both the tangible and intangible aspects, as well as the implications of any course of action.

While decision making is the process that leads to actionable conclusions, critical thinking is the element that defines whether the choice is sound.[8]

Intuitive thinking is the ability to take what you may sense or perceive to be true and, without knowledge or evidence, appropriately factor it into the final decision.

So why would anyone even choose to put the energy into thinking?

WHAT MOTIVATES PEOPLE TO THINK?

In the same way we can have our powers of intuition trained out of us, we can also have our motivation to think trained out of us. Consider these three types of attitudes toward thinking:[9] being naïve, selfish, or fair-minded.

Prairie Chicken Pippin—Values being naïve

Consider the person who doesn't think they need to think, like our friend Pippin. Pippin generally feels content that he already understands things and doesn't value spending time to figure things out, because someone else will eventually do that for him. He believes most of what he sees and hears regardless of the source and is not inclined to question what he hears. He knows other people around him will take care of him, especially if he shows distress. He does what he is told and goes along with what his peer group is doing. Pippin embraces the status quo and feels he might get into trouble if he rocks the boat. Pippin has no intention to hurt anyone, but also assumes no one would intend to harm him. The kind of thinking Pippin practices, and its results, look like this:

- Pippin is a ready victim for more sophisticated

manipulators due to his lack of awareness of pending trouble or controversy.

- Pippin will make mistakes because he doesn't know how to monitor what he hears for accuracy of interpretation.
- Wherever mindless obedience succeeds, he will get by.
- *Pippin's most practiced thinking skill is how to entice others to do the thinking.*

Scammin' Cam—Values being selfish

Now consider the person who thinks for the purpose of getting what they want, even if it's at the expense of others. Let's call her Cam. Cam likes to think of ways to trick people to get what she wants. She knows how to get around people of authority and how to manipulate others to do her bidding. She is excellent at argument and debate. She tells people what they want to hear in order to stay clear of facing consequences. The kind of thinking Cam practices looks like this:

- Cam does understand the power of figuring things out for herself (unlike Pippin).
- Cam knows what she wants and figures out what is standing in the way of that.
- Cam cares only about those who serve her, those who are members of her group. She understands the advantages to gain by becoming a leader and exercising control over others.
- *Cam's most practiced thinking skill is how to successfully put her desires above the needs and rights of others.*

Wise Winn—Values being fair-minded

Finally, consider a person who thinks for the purpose of learning to understand themselves *and* others. Let me introduce you to Wise Winn. Winn notices that people don't always do what they say and knows he can't always believe what he hears or learns from various information sources. Winn acknowledges that people say things they don't mean when they are trying to please others. Winn wants to make things better for everyone, not just his group. Winn recognizes that to understand people, you must understand their situation. Winn knows it's *easier* to be naïve (like Pippin) or selfish (like Cam), yet he still holds himself accountable to be fair with others because that's how he expects others to treat him. You might say Winn is a cognitively virtuous citizen.

> A cognitively virtuous citizen thinks for the purpose of understanding themselves and others to make things better for everyone.

The kind of thinking Winn practices looks like this:

- Winn knows he can solve problems and do difficult things.
- Winn can express himself and create meaningful relationships.
- Winn learned how to enter the thinking of other people and see things from their perspective.
- *Winn notices the need to protect himself and people like Pippin from the Cams of the world without violating the rights of others.*

Now, what is critical thinking all about? I am suggesting it's about having the right attitude towards thinking. As Winn shows us, it's hard to think, and it's even harder to think with fairness for everyone involved! So what's the payoff? Why expend so much energy thinking?

WHAT KIND OF THINKING WILL YOU PRACTICE?

In the end, I feel critical thinking is about being accountable for how you process information and being a positive contributor to your community. If you do your work in thinking, others don't have to spend energy picking up after messes *you* decided to make.

Critical thinking is about guarding yourself from being gullible and naïve. Gullibility is a failure of social intelligence in which a person is easily tricked or manipulated into an ill-advised course of action (like Pippin is likely to do). This can hurt Pippin as well as place a burden on those around him.

Critical thinking is about not confusing correctness with what's popular, or quality with what's popular (like Cam is likely to do). This puts the Cams of the community in a position to take advantage of others (like poor Pippin again) who have the tendency to believe unlikely propositions that are unsupported by evidence.

Critical thinking is also about striving for what is right and true to your values, and you're not going to find non-biased, third-party-provided data on that. You have to look within.

One of the issues to consider is how your decision will potentially impact other people. Think about what value that has in terms of your belief system and what you're trying to achieve, and incorporate that into your decision-making.

Dr. Mehran Sahami, Advisory board for the
McCoy Family Center for Ethics in Society[10]

It is your obligation to encourage yourself and those around you to adopt an attitude toward thinking that supports a healthy self-image, builds confidence, grows acceptance and trustworthiness, generates gratitude and is based on joy.

To some degree we all have to live with the decisions those around us make; the ripples start small, but the absolutely go wide. It's a valuable contribution to simply help ourselves make successful decisions we feel happy to own. In this way, we adopt a practice of accountability for the results.

When we grow trust in applying intuition to our decisions, we give ourselves permission to use the advantages inherent with intuition. In the end, this benefits everyone.

Cultivating our ability to trust what is right within ourselves is more important now than ever. With the technology around us today, we can easily and immediately observe each other—our words, our opinions, our choices.

> During the simple act of observation, the energy of our words, opinions and choices is transformed to effect very real change the world.

Have you ever Tweeted, posted on Instagram or Facebook? Posts are observed, and you know it affects change. Remember that woman and the Chewbacca mask?[11a] Her joyful birthday indulgence not only made millions of people smile, it made retailers a bunch of money too! Go ahead, take a few minutes, click that link and enjoy.

Yes, you can, and you are, changing the world.

So, I encourage you to be a cognitively virtuous citizen, *right now!*

Do your best to ensure your impact, your energy, contributes to our world in a positive way. Just take a small extra moment to check in and see if that choice you are about to make is informed by critical thinking, motivated by joy, and has an attitude of fair-mindedness.

The practices suggested in this book may just provide what is needed to help you over the hurdles of indecision and onto action that aligns with your values. Of course, there is no guarantee for improving the *outcome* of your decisions (we cover that in the next chapter) but if you make the effort and take to heart the strategies and practices, you will be making decisions that result in less surprise endings, less opportunity for regret, and more opportunity for bringing the changes you want into your life and the lives of those around you.

CHAPTER · 2

GOOD DECISIONS BAD OUTCOMES

Indecision isn't just uncomfortable and annoying. In fact, it's been said that indecision assassinates innovation, and that indecision is an indicator of an unsuccessful person. It is known that indecision is a very real cognitive symptom of people with major depression.[11]

Indecision is when decision making is delayed or even avoided. Basically, you feel stuck.

We make decisions every day. According to Dr. Eva Krockow,[12] sources say we make around 2,000 decision an hour (yes, that is not a typo, two thousand decisions per hour!). Generally, we don't think about this decision-making process. We just automatically do it.

So what is it about some decisions that makes it so difficult to move forward?

CHOICE NOT CHORE

Have you ever found yourself in a position where you felt there were no options? I think having equally bad options feels like no options. Sure, we've all been there: the old adage is "between a rock and a hard place." Homer provides some great visualization of this situation when he describes Odysseus's sailing options as confronting a six-headed monster or a deadly whirlpool, "caught between Scylla and Charybdis." Or my personal favorite: "jumping from the frying pan into the fire"—it's all hot and it all hurts. It's easy to see why you wouldn't want even try to make a decision, you would just let the current situation keep on keeping on. Why even bother attempting change?

There is no getting around the reality that we face dilemmas all the time. There are studies that tell us we make 35,000 decisions a day. The struggle is real! How often have you been faced with these:

- Should I do what's right or what's easy?
- Pay now or pay later?
- Follow my family traditions or go outside that and follow what brings me personal fulfillment and growth?
- Do it the expert way or my way?

A place to begin is to frame your thinking in terms of *choice* and not *decision*. It's more than semantics, but just considering where these words come from.

The origin of the word *decision* is from 15th century French meaning literally "to cut off," or "final judgment."

The origin of *choice*, from 12th century French, is "the act of selecting," "to discern;" and from Old English *cyre*, "free will."

When facing a tough decision, you are going to be more inclined to have the motivation needed to bring about change and own the results if you feel you are exercising free will, right? It's about engaging in your situation, being in the moment, and choosing to be involved. Like my yoga teacher says, it's choice not chore.

Svetlana Whitener suggests that effective decision making can only flow from a place of choice.[13] I would add to that notion that intuition plays its role from a place of choice.

26

Effective decision making can only flow from a place of choice. Personal choice is where our intuition blooms.

There is always a choice when you put yourself in a choice-making frame of mind. When you make a decision (or a choice) that's not the end, there is no "final" in the act of making a decision; the decision is the thing that kicks of the beginning of action. In our own experience, and I think we have all had this, once the choice or decision is made, it feels like a weight off our shoulders and we then we are free to move forward.

Letting Go

If we consider some of the toughest decisions we make in our lives, chances are they have to do with letting something go.

Letting go of a friend, of a job, of a home or a neighborhood; letting go of something we previously believed in, of habitual patterns. When a tough decision presents itself we instinctively know this impact, and that's not always something we feel up to facing.

Of course, the reason behind all this consternation is a nagging want, a desire to bring about change. Counseling ourselves to let go and move on is really just part of the decision-making process.

I had an interesting interaction with a client I worked with years ago. I was hired to help his organization identify why their digital production was mysteriously exceedingly slow. We were tasked to establish incremental improvements to the process including new ways to measure and report production metrics. This was a big change for them since no one was really sure what the process even was in its entirety, and historically very few production measurements and metrics were defined. They just watched the output trends over time and recognized they were not up to snuff with common industry expectations.

We did a very enlightening opening exercise with the team where we walked around the room, shook hands with everyone, introduced ourselves, and included in our introduction *what we are really thinking in our head but typically wouldn't say out loud* . . . but said it out loud anyway.

Me: (thinking how much I hate these icebreakers) Hi, I'm Terrie, the systems analyst on the team, and I really don't like icebreakers much.

Teammate #1: Nice to meet you, Terrie. I am Jake, your subject matter expert, and I'm really quite introverted, and pretty uncomfortable being here right now.

Me: (making a mental note about Jake and how to best approach future interactions, now shaking hands with teammate #2) Huh, this icebreaker may have more value than I originally thought. I'm Terrie the systems analyst.

Teammate #2: Hi Terrie, I am Sue and I can't wait to get out of this kick-off and get on to the *real* work.

Me: (thinking about how I like the openness of this group, reaching out my hand to the next person but he speaks first) . . .

Executive Sponsor and Decision Maker: Hi, I'm Nick, and I know you are the analyst on the team, but I already know more on this topic than you will be able to figure out during this project.

Me: (a bit aghast, but then somewhat appreciative of this reveal) Well

Nick, it is nice to meet you. I am Terrie and I will partner with the subject matter experts you trust most to ensure the findings and recommendations we bring for your consideration have a meaningful impact.

I immediately felt the thinking whirlwind that came with cognitive dissonance.

Try-to-tease-it-apart me: So our decision maker thought he already knew how this was going to go. I, on the other hand, *am pretty sure* I will find something no one has ever thought of before. Hmmm.

Self-doubting me: Wait, maybe I don't have the right background to be successful on this project.

Smug me: Huh, yeah, we'll see, Mr. I-already-know.

Mind-reading me: Did he just say he didn't want to hear from me?

Exit-stage-left me: Do I need to look into participating with a different work group?

Brain-shifting me: I need to discover how set our sponsor is in his preconceived notions and find out if his ideas are founded on real data or not. If he's totally dug in, it would be a huge endeavor to get a shift.

Risk-planning me: We may have to plan time to implement what he already 'knows' and then put the fruit of our analysis into the second release.

So that became an option for how to move forward, but one thing I knew for sure: to bring about this change, we both were going to have to loosen the grip on our initial biased and limiting beliefs.

You Can't Stop Bias & Fallacy

Dan Ariely, a behavior economist, uses a common visual illusion as a metaphor for rationality.[14] The two tables in the diagram are the same in dimension. Go ahead and hold up something to measure with right now and convince yourself: indeed, the left table is the same length as the right table.

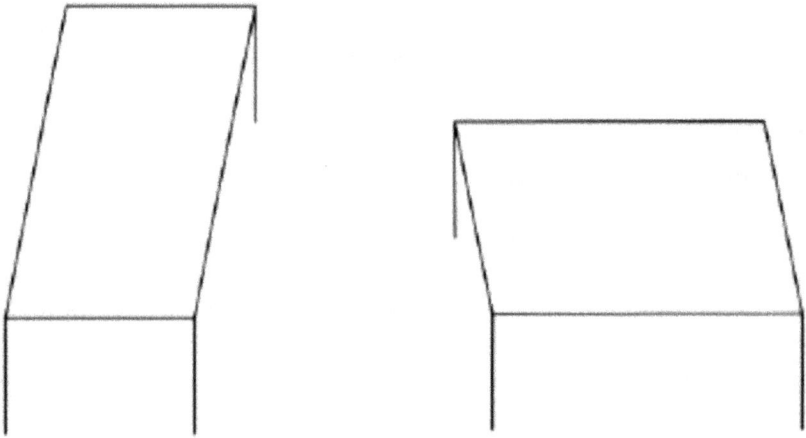

The weird thing is, even after you measure it, you can't stop seeing the left table as longer. "It's like you haven't learned anything," Ariely says. Even though we have an entire part of our brain dedicated to thinking about seeing, every time we look at these we come out with the wrong idea: an illusion about reality. Turns out we fall into this thinking trap a lot: as of this writing, Wikipedia has a list of 86 optical illusions.[15]

What our thinking does when we make decisions is prone to a similar kind of cognitive trap. Cognitive biases (or cognitive illusions) are errors in our thinking that lead us astray from making rational judgments: we can't help ourselves from applying intuition to jump to conclusions.

Our intuition is really fooling us in a repeatable, predictable, consistent way, there is almost nothing we can do about it.

Dan Ariely, Founder of the Center
forAdvanced Hindsight

So how prone are we to this kind of thinking trap? According to Wikipedia, there are 188 cognitive illusions for us to fall into! Take a moment and look at this nice infographic of all the cognitive bias as visualized by Svisualcapatalist.com.[16]

Some of these biases are especially impactful to decision making where the desirability of options is part of the illusion. For example, take the Status Quo Bias, where the tendency is to like things to stay relatively the same. Familiarity and comfort are so tasty! Right?! Why rock the boat? The Bandwagon Effect is something we see every day: the tendency to do, or think, things because all those other people do (what would Prairie Chicken Pippin do?).

We also know the way information is presented makes a difference in the way people interpret it. Marketing professions exploit this all the time. You don't even have to be all that creative; just present something over and over and you have evoked the Mere-Exposure Effect. This is one of the most commonly used cognitive-bias bait techniques, and most people don't even know they are using it. This is the tendency to like and develop trust in things we see as familiar. So the more we see it, the more we believe it to be trustworthy. Clearly, repeated exposure is not a real trust-building method, it's just our brain tricking us again.

But wait, there's more!

Intermixed in many of the lists of biases are *fallacies*. Fallacies are very related to biases but distinctly different. Daniel Kahneman (who literally wrote *the* book on cognitive bias) describes fallacies like this:

The word fallacy is used, in general, when people fail to apply a logical rule that is obviously relevant. Fallacies are related to cognitive biases, arising from our brain's same tendency to take mental shortcuts (often called heuristics) in making decisions or answering questions. As logical as you think you are, your brain deals better with intuition than logic.

Daniel Kahneman,
2002 Nobel Prize in Economics

Take the Hot-Hand Fallacy: this is the irrational belief that if you win several chance games in a row; you are 'hot,' meaning that the streak is likely to continue, as if it has something to do with more than pure probability. You don't have to be a professional gambler to relate to this one: one afternoon playing the board game Aggravation with my mom and brother, I learned to embrace the glory and disgrace of this illusion!

With the multitude of ways our own thinking is leading us to ir-rational decisions (this is a 'bad' way to make decisions), when are we ever really making our own, non-biased, 'good' decisions? Ariely tells us that many of our decisions are not really from within us, but that we often have an *illusion* of making a decision.

Wait, what?

Right from the start, we are subject to our *own* cognitive bias. Then on top of that, we also have a tendency to *allow others* to make decisions for us. Even when we do have a choice.

Why do we do this?

It's because we care. It's difficult and it's complex. It's so complex that we don't know what to do. And because we have no idea what to do, we just pick whatever it was that was chosen for us.

Daniel Ariely

Personalization Technology and Social Bias

The way we enjoy getting information is one more thing that is working against our ability to make rational decisions. We tend to evaluate information more favorably when it comes from our own social community because a set of ideas and beliefs is reinforced within the group. So certain conclusions will 'win,' but only because the incoming information is one-sided. This selective way of receiving information doesn't allow for much alternative thinking or competing beliefs. Social media platform users might see their feed turning into this kind of "echo chamber," reinforcing cognitive and social bias, isolating people from a diversity of information.[17]

To make matters worse, we know that social media posted content is of questionable accuracy; anyone can post and anyone can claim to be an expert backed with credible data. Oh, and don't forget, about 15% of Twitter accounts show signs of being bots![18] This means the content is a mix of correct information, misinformation (incorrect information) and disinformation (intentionally false information).

Putting it all together, our well-groomed social feed we've been honing in on for years can be jamming an echo chamber of low-credibility sources into our already biased thinking.

What about when we reference what is trending? Algorithms designed to promote popular content—that's Popularity Bias at its finest, reinforcing what appears to be popular irrespective of the quality of the information. And it's not only social media platforms but also search engine algorithms that control results, returning only the information that would be most engaging to you.

Personalization technologies are designed to select the most engaging and relevant content for each individual user. But in doing so, it may end up reinforcing the cognitive and social biases of users, making them vulnerable to manipulation.

Giovanni Luca Ciampagli, assistant professor of Computer Science[19]

How do I even begin to think critically, with an attitude of fair-mindedness, and use my intuition to know what is right?

Basically, it's a matter of developing some discipline around managing your own bias.

To start with, when you search the internet for information and solution options, don't just keep looking around until you find data that agrees with your own preconceived notions. That's indulging in Confirmation Bias, which is looking for information that supports our beliefs rather than for evidence suggesting we are wrong.

For a funny illustration of this bias in action, watch on YouTube *If Google was a Guy Part 5*. At 1:15, the researcher is looking for "Climate change not real." There was a huge amount of information to support the fact that climate change *is real*, but she pressed on to find the small piece of information that agreed with her own belief that it wasn't, and happily left the scene completely validated. The anti-vax movement is another example: the World Health Organization has identified vaccine hesitancy as one of the top 10 threats to global health in 2019. "The reluctance or refusal to vaccinate despite the availability of vaccines . . . one of the most cost-effective ways of avoiding disease." Lack of confidence in a vaccine is noted as a key reason for vaccine hesitancy. Confirmation bias can be problematic in a *big* way.

So what else can you do when considering reliable information sources?[20]

- Read the story, not just the headline
- Notice who wrote the piece
- If it sounds unbelievable, look it up
- Don't just follow people who agree with you

CAN I EVEN MAKE AN EFFECTIVE DECISION?

After learning about everything that can trip us up in decision making, you may be asking yourself, so what is an *effective* decision?

How do I do it right?

Dan Gilbert, a Harvard psychologist, gives a TED talk[21] where he describes how Daniel Bournoulii gave mankind the gift of an equation for "How to Do Exactly the Right Thing at All Possible Times"

$$E(u \mid p, X) = \Sigma_{x \in} X \, p(x)u(x)$$

The idea this equation describes is, the benefit we can count on getting out of a decision is the product of the *odds of gaining something* and the *value of that gain to us.*

Expected Value = (Odds of Gain) X (Value of Gain)

So, if we can estimate and multiply these two things we will always know what to do. But, Gilbert goes on to describe, we humans are bad at estimating probability and value of success. We, just by being human, are prone to applying thinking flaws. Sorry, we are going to need more than this equation.

How about all those times we made decisions and things turned out really great? Can we just replicate the way we made that decision? Oh, if only it was that easy.

We tend to think if the outcome was good, the decision was good.

But, according to Danial Kahneman (the Nobel Laureate who told us decisions are a gamble) when it comes to decision making you can't really tell if you made a good or bad decision.

A good decision, the best possible decision can have bad outcomes and a bad decision can have good outcomes.

Daniel Kahneman

He goes on to explain that judging by outcomes is a problem. It is related to the cognitive bias of hindsight (yeah, another one of those thinking flaws we can't help ourselves from). Hindsight causes us to make unjust decisions.

As an uplifting way to look at it, you can't really make the wrong decision! But you can sure go about deciding the wrong way!

You can't really make a wrong decision. But you sure can go about deciding in the wrong way.

When you realize a bad outcome, a question you may ask yourself is, is this because I made a bad (irrational) decision, or did I simply make a mistake?

Here's an example of what I mean. I moved from Florida to California and had to take a written test to get a California driver's license.

I remember *consciously choosing to not study* for this annoying but necessary test. My reasoning behind this choice went like this:

Expert me: For crying out loud, I have been driving for twenty years, I understand the rules of the road.

Ignorant me: How different can driving in California really be? It's still the United States, the sign symbols are the same, I can read and figure things out.

Saving-time me: I am wasting enough time as it is with going to the DMV for this, so I will minimize my time invested and just go straight in and take the test.

Efficient planner me: In the very unlikely case that I fail it, I will already be in the DMV. I can pick up the book, take another get-in-line ticket, read the book while waiting for my turn, and then retest and get my license.

Fast forward to what really happened. I failed the test, and the

California licensing rules said I couldn't retest until at least a week later. Now I had put myself in the embarrassing and time-consuming position of having to do the whole dang process twice. Where did I go wrong?

The choice to not study was an irrational decision; it was a bad decision AND it had bad results.

- I didn't have complete information about California licensing rules.
- I had an incorrect assumption about their driving guidelines being the same as Florida.
- I completely did not even consider the weighting California put on memorizing the nuances of driving under the influence of alcohol.
- I had complete ignorance of the wait-a-week-to-retest rule.

Bottom line: my arrogance in jumping to the conclusion that I already knew everything to pass the test biased me so wholeheartedly that I didn't do proper information gathering or make even one phone call to confirm my assumptions. I didn't even give myself *a chance* to make a good, well-informed decision.

Now, when I picked the wrong answers during the test, that was just making simple mistakes.

I didn't intentionally pick the wrong answers, so at least *that* part of the whole experience was not a bad decision, just good ol' fashioned honest mistake-making.

I was slimed by cognitive bias! It was all over me and it led to irrational thinking, negatively affecting my reasoning around studying.

How can you recognize when your decision making had errors in it?

Remember, we can't just look at the *outcome*, but there are some "bad" things we can observe.

Twelve Symptoms of a Flawed Decision

- I am not sure if the results address the problem.
- I didn't take the time to understand my current situation and preferences before I evaluated options.
- I didn't have a process to follow: I might have jumped to conclusions before getting enough information.
- I freaked out, so I didn't do anything.
- I didn't have an objective person I trust to share my thinking and bounce ideas with.
- I didn't validate the assumptions I had.
- My search for information was shallow, biased or off-topic.
- I didn't consider many (or any) options.
- I did not understand the risks or impacts of the options I selected.
- I never reconsidered the options I rejected.
- I never envisioned what it would be like to live with the results.
- I didn't have much confidence in my decision or never imagined a contingency plan.

If you're seeing some of these things crop up in your decision making, it's time to start building your own bias-busting tool kit!

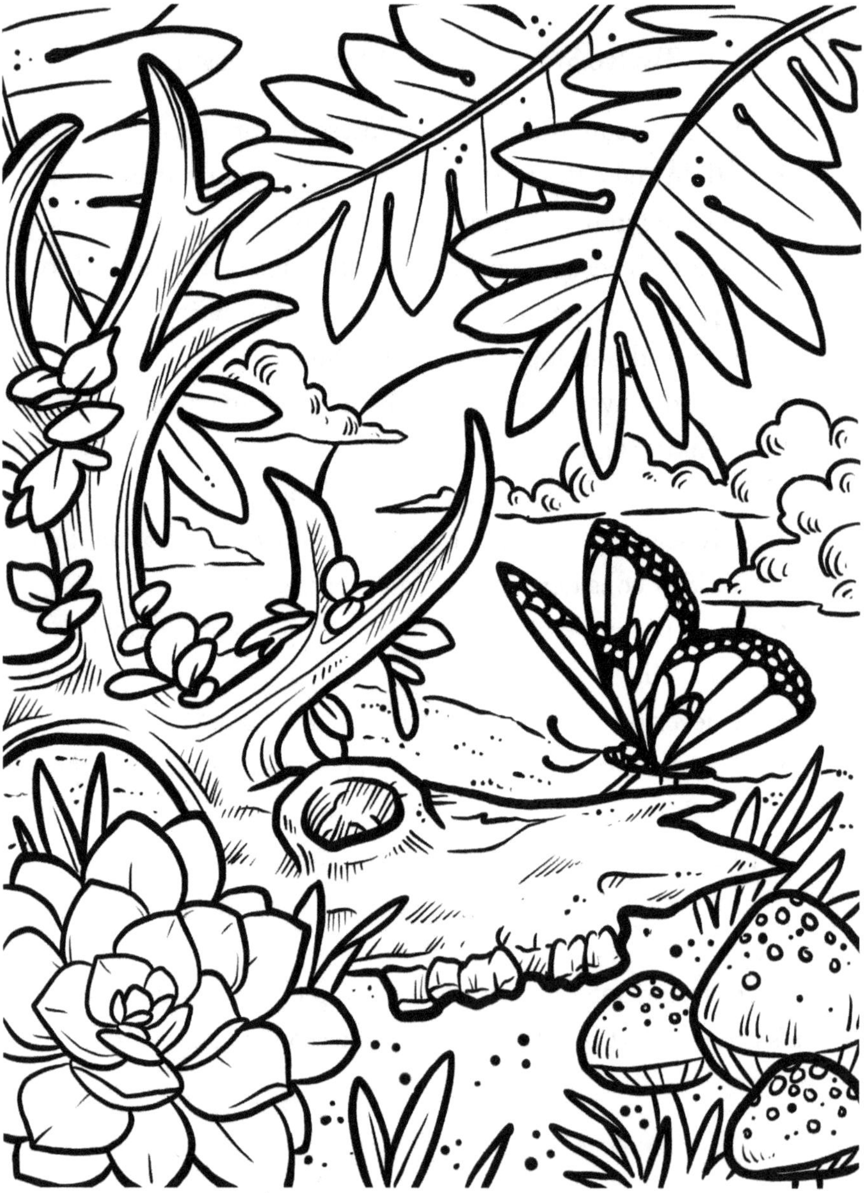

CHAPTER · 3

You Vs. Brain Bias: How to Win the Battle of Cognitive Illusions

Trust-Me Notebook

Before we get going, it's worth mentioning that you are going to need a trusty notebook. I call it a "Trust-Me" notebook, because when I write down things about how I am making choices, over time, it helps me build confidence in my choice-making abilities. I can review what I was thinking (without the bias of hindsight!) and use that as information when various hard decisions come up the next time.

I left a little writing space at various places here in this book (yes, permission to write in the book, and color in the book for that matter, but that comes a bit later!). You can use this to start with, but you're going to want to keep something that can grow over time. We will talk more about that in the section about cultivating dexterity in quality choice making. What we will focus on here is using writing things down as a tool to help you neutralize the effect of cognitive illusions.

A Space to Breathe

One more simple thing that will make a big difference in your thinking and choice-making practice is a designated space to un-think. I call it a "Space to Breathe" because this is where I give myself permission to take a moment to let thoughts settle with no rush or distractions: just me, breathing, some gentle thinking, and maybe a little writing or drawing. I happen to have a designated thinking chair. It's cozy and I like being there. I also consider my car a thought settling space. Most every night, my shower is a space to let my thoughts fly around a bit until they go down the drain and my brain is nice and fresh when I towel off. I like to shower before I write. Listening to music is a fantastic space to breathe for me. It offers a rhythm for breathing and moving, exactly what is needed to settle thoughts and make room for creativity. The point is, if you don't already have a space like this, find one. If already have places like this, acknowledge them and prioritize being there regularly.

Take a Walk

My neighborhood walking path and my workplace walking path are frequently my Spaces to Breathe.

According to a 2017 Stanford University study, published in the *Journal of Experimental Psychology: Learning, Memory, and Cognition*, walking encourages "divergent thinking" where this pattern of thought is understood to bring original ideas to the problem. In other words, walking increases your creativity, and can improve business outcomes by helping you come up with more and better ideas.[22] It's been used by everyone from philosophers to business leaders. You get the idea: while making difficult decisions or thinking through complex problems, not only wisdom but research shows walking truly makes a positive difference.

Be Curious!

When we are curious, we view tough situations more creatively.

Francesca Gino, behavioral scientist[23]

In simple terms, curiosity is when you just want to go and learn new things. Curiosity is said to involve four dimensions of thinking:[24]

- Creativity and problem solving
- Distress tolerance
- Openness to new ideas and to viewing things from different perspectives
- Inquisitiveness

A study[25] in *Neuron* magazine suggests that as you become curious, the brain's chemistry changes, in turn helping you to retain information and increase your learning. The brain provides a nice bit of dopamine to encourage you to continue the quest; you experience wonder and awe—the emotional signatures of curiosity.

According to the research by Francesca Geno, when curiosity is triggered we are less likely to fall prey to confirmation bias and to stereotyping people. Since highly curious people tend to consume more varied information, they are less likely to have a one-sided perspective. On the other hand, low-curiosity people opt for familiar evidence consistent with what they already believe.[26] That's right, simple curiosity goes straight for the jugular of confirmation bias!

A great way to reduce decision-making errors is simply to be curious about the topic at hand.

If being curious isn't already part of your way of being, it is widely agreed that you can't *learn* how to be curious, but you can make the time and give yourself the freedom to nurture your curiosity. Try it out and practice it. I highly encourage you to adopt curiosity as part of your thinking practice.

ESTABLISH YOUR SELF-KNOWLEDGE BASELINE

The best place to start when approaching a decision is to take time and recognize what is important to you. Give yourself permission to take a moment and focus on self-knowledge.

Maybe you are thinking you already know yourself and don't need to waste time on this. Remember the thinking attitude of Prairie Chicken Pippin? When you are facing a big problem and all the decisions that go with that, now is not the time for mindless obedience and presenting yourself as a target for sophisticated manipulators! Let's do this!

Have you taken the time to sit down with yourself and ask—What do I believe? Why do I believe it? What do I want to believe? Who do I trust? What makes me tick? We're not very good at asking ourselves, but you know who is? Con artists.

Maria Konnikova, psychology expert-turned-poker champion[27]

Begin by understanding what you want from solving the problem. When you consider this, you will develop a clear understanding of the change you want.

Be sure to write down in your Trust-me notebook everything you discover in your self-knowledge exploration.

Know the problem

Ask yourself to describe the problem fully. You may feel like you can skip this and go right to what you want. Don't go there just yet. I can't tell you how many times in my professional experience the client has invested in pursing what they want, only to find, what they built didn't address the root of the problem. It's so tempting to put energy in describing the solution before putting energy into describing the need. But we got this! Start with a deep understanding of the problem.

- What is the problem?
- Does this problem have a story that has taken place over a span of time?
- Is this my problem? How can I tell it's my problem?
- Will this problem go away on its own? Have I ignored it before? Why is this time different?
- Is there a time or day I need to have this problem solved by?
- Did this problem surprise me? What was surprising about it? What was annoyingly familiar about it?
- What emotions does this problem bring up in me? In those around me?

The point here is to look within and make friends with the problem; get to know it as well as you can.

✎ Enter what the problem really is in your Trust-Me notebook

Make friends with the fear

That last question about emotions—it's a lulu, and worth digging into a little. Understanding what emotions this problem creates in you may mean it is time to face your fears.

The need for change typically arrives for one of two reasons: either we want to *proactively* make change happen, or we are *reacting* to a change that is directly impacting us. In either case we all know change isn't easy, and when we are reacting to something unexpected one of our initial reactions is typically fear.

I call this initial fear moment "The Freak-out."

My stage-zero cervical cancer diagnosis came with a full-blown freak-out. My thoughts spun round, I thought everything I was feeling and doing was wrong. Every thought seemed like a direct route to a declining lifestyle until the inevitable bitter end.

My advice about dealing with a Freak-out? Give yourself a reasonable timeframe to just let it all spill out: it should be as long as what's reasonable for you. In the movies they say you get one tear, but for me it takes a least a day. That said, I wouldn't let it go on for more than, say, a couple days.

Here's the important part: as it unfolds—*take notice*, because your fear tells you what you value, believe and find joy in.

Freaking out?
Give yourself a timeframe of a couple days to let it all spill out.
Take notice of what is revealed.
Your fear tells you what you value, believe and find joy in.

Here's what my two-day HPV diagnosis freak-out looked like:

Shamed me: Should I not talk about this to anyone?

Analyzing me: Is that shame I am feeling? This is, after all, in part caused by a sexually transmitted disease. Will people think I am not a good person?

Hover-Mom me: How will this affect my kids? My parents? I want to be a role model for my kids and my family. I want them to know this challenge I am facing is not a secret, nor something to sweep under the rug, nor something to be ashamed of. *I want my family to be at peace when they think about my health and well-being.*

Bad-idea me: Should I hide it from them?

Unworthy me: Do I deserve this? I *have* chosen to have multiple partners as a lifestyle, after all . . .

Judging me: Was that wrong? Maybe remaining single and continuing to pursue intimate relationships really is too risky.

Analyzing me: Why am I avoiding the doctor's treatment suggestion? Am I foolish to not just follow the most conservative/aggressive treatment plans to avoid progression of cancer? I am, after all, *old*. I am certainly not going to have another baby. Am I holding on too tight to body parts that just don't really matter anymore?

Jumping-to-conclusions me: Will I never have pleasurable sex again? It took me fifty years to discover cervical orgasms and I am not giving that up without a fight. The intimacy in my current relationship is a huge part of what makes me feel alive.

Crystal-ball me: Should I start mentally, physically and financially preparing for the progression of having my body parts removed? The likelihood of chemo?

Conspiracy-theory me: Why do they even call it 'stage-zero cancer'? That term seems like an evil plot to brainwash a large number of women into predetermining for themselves that things may go in a bad direction so they seek out extra screenings and services that feed into the corrupt insurance system. Is that why he didn't offer even a single alternative treatment option?

Freak-out me: Is it possible to stop worrying about this? Ever? Is this just who I am now? A person going down the path of dealing with cancer?

It didn't really just stop at the self-talk either. The freak-out leaked onto other people I love and trust. Which was a good thing, because then they could lift me up with love and encouragement. Like my yoga teacher would say, "Oh fear! Take my hand! Let's be friends!"

Know your values, beliefs and what you find joy in

Your values and beliefs and joys are the guide you need to frame your decisions moving forward into the change you want to bring about.

After the freak-out, take what spilled out and now apply your curiosity. What was the fearful thought revealing?

Here are the things I discovered were important to me, just by poking at my fearful thoughts.

- I value honesty and open communication, especially with my family.
- I need to see myself as healthy, and my family to see the same.

48

- I would not tolerate allowing myself to feel shame for being in this situation.
- I believe I am underserved as a woman if I allow removal of my cervix (or any body part for that matter) before it's necessary.

You will notice an amazing power when you observe the energy in your fears.

✎ Enter what you value in your Trust-Me notebook

In physics, the observer effect is a theory that simply by observing energy, the energy is changed, transformed into a new form of energy. Creating change through observation, it's a thing. If you watch an electron, the electron changes its behavior. If you watch a person, they change their behavior (Hawthorne effect). If you watch your fear, it changes into your values and beliefs.[28]

> If you watch your fear, it changes your values and beliefs.

Know what success looks like

Set the stage for a good decision

From previous discussion we discovered a few things:
- It's essential to include intuition in decisions when the intent is to bring about sustainable change.
- Effective decision making comes from a place of choice.
- Thinking is done with an attitude of fair-mindedness.

Okay. Those are the *perquisites* going into decision making, but how I can tell a decision is good?

What a good decision will do for you

When a decision is successful, here's what it will do for you:

- The decision addresses the problem.
- The decision instills confidence: you know the work and the results are possible and desirable. This doesn't necessarily mean the work is in your comfort zone! But that's OK.
- All impacts of the decision are understood: when the results are in, there are not really any surprises. This will remove the opportunity for blame and regret!

A successful decision:
Addresses the problem
Instills confidence
Identifies related impacts

Visualizing *your* results

Once you've taken the time to look inside of you to define what you believe and value, it becomes clear to you what criteria needs to be met in your solution options and it's time to start envisioning the end game. My favorite question for defining success is, "What will you see when this turns out wildly successful?"

What will you see when this turns out wildly successful?

- What will you have/not have? Is there something you want so deeply you just know it's going to happen?
- When do you think you will have that?
- How will you see yourself?
- How will others see you?
- How will you feel?
- Who will you be thanking?
- What will your life look once you have absorbed the results into your day-to-day activities?

I want to emphasize that there is no textbook right answer for what success is for you. Be extremely honest in saying what you want! Some of my past clients' success expectations sounded like this:

I know this is successful when:

- I won't have to deal with the constant stream of confused-people phone calls.
- I will no longer hear that barking dog.
- All the 'easy' items are delivered, so my team gains confidence.
- I won't be afraid to walk across the room and get my day hijacked by a person with a broken workstation calling me over.
- I won't have to listen to teams argue about whose fault it is.
- I will understand if doubling the sales staff will be the significant factor in reaching our growth target.

🖊 Enter what success looks like in your Trust-Me notebook

ACCEPT WHERE YOU ARE NOW

It's important to have solid understanding of your current situation.

This is about acknowledging what is going on right now, inside of you and around you. Honest observation of your current circumstance will help you understand what will affect your ability to realistically move forward. After you decide what you will have, you also need to fully believe it is possible you can have it.

Current-situation observation is not difficult, since it's things you already know and do right now. The trick is to notice it, as it is—not how you wish it to be, or how you previously thought it was. Not even how you previously told people about it; just come to grips with now, exactly as it is.

One thing we know now is that we must work with those pesky cognitive biases and fallacies we are so prone to. We may even have some prejudices right now that are getting in our way of progress. We will have to work with those too.

Did I say it's not difficult? Ha! Well, seeing it might not be that hard, but accepting things as they are can really challenge us.

When looking at and accepting your current situation, you may have to update your values and beliefs list, because acceptance will ultimately reveal what you believe in.

Here are some things to ask yourself:

- How do you take care of yourself? Observe your own habits in eating, exercising, re-energizing, your work and home environment, finances, your safety and medical care.
- Define any constraints or boundaries you must work within that you have limited or no control over. Are there people you must or must not work with on this? Do you have a

"due date" on making a decision, or realizing the result? Do you have financial constraints?

- Is there anything about yourself or your situation that you typically don't share with others? Observe what you avoid communicating with people you trust and love, co-workers, strangers. Note why you do that, the results you observe, and your feelings.
- Are you concerned this might be the last chance to do or say something important to you? Why is it important? Note why you haven't done it so far and how you feel.

Once you can articulate what you observe about how things really are, then you can consider if you need or want to change anything to be able to move forward.

- Is there anything you may need to let go of?
- Maybe something new you need to start doing?
- Are there things you need to continue doing no matter what?
- Do you believe that is possible?

Acceptance will also help you realize your superpowers or the power of the situation around you.

- Is there something about yourself that is just going to shine no matter what? How cool is that?
- Is there something about the people or the places around you that will affect your ability to move forward? In a positive or negative way?

🖊 Enter what you must accept about your current situation in your Trust-Me notebook

SELF-KNOWLEDGE SUMMARY

Congratulations on taking the time and energy to recognize what is important to you! You will go into your big decision knowing what you want. This is seriously no small achievement. I highly encourage you to jot down what you have observed about yourself right now!

You will come back to these, as they will provide some guard-rails for option evaluation which will significantly increase your commitment to doing the hard work of moving your plan to bring about change forward.

🖊 My understanding of the problem—the cause for change

_____

🖊 My friendship with fear revealed this!

_____

🖊 My values and beliefs

_____

🖊 My vision of success—the desired change

_____

🖊 My current situation—what I need to accept

_____

Ask What Would You Have Your Best Friend Do?

It turns out that people choose differently when it is for themselves versus someone else.[29]

When we choose for ourselves, we tend to be more reserved, cautious and risk-averse, deep-diving into a narrower set of information. When we choose for others, we tend to explore more numerous options and focus on overall impressions, applying more creativity and boldness. So what does this mean if you want to improve your decision-making practice? Distance yourself from your own problem using a mental exercise: ask yourself (refer to yourself in the third person), "What should *you* do?" Or imagine yourself as a different person, someone you look up to or respect as a good decision maker, and visualize what decision *they* would make.

Have a Decision Coach

The deal is this: because cognitive illusions are so much a part of us, you just can't recognize your own bias! One of the best things you can do is have a decision coach there alongside you, helping to check if bias is being introduced into your decision making. Now, that's not the full extent of what you will want your decision coach to help you with: generally, to get the most bang for your buck from a decision coach, you'll want them by your side through the entire experience. A decision coach can be there for you before, during and after the change you want to bring into the world.

First and foremost, your decision coach is *your* advocate, encouraging you and helping to fulfill *your* specific desires.

Upon mutual agreement, your coach may:

- Answer questions about the decision-making and transformation process
- Help you understand techniques, procedures and complexities
- Help you develop a plan that serves to bring your vision to reality
- Help communicate your preferences to everyone involved in your change effort
- Prepare you for how to own the results, including any "care and feeding" or maintenance involved
- When desired, your coach can help perform activities and tasks in the plan that moves you forward to your goal

Your decision coach *is* a person who:

- You trust
- Critiques decision making—bringing you feedback as close to real-time as possible. The coach should be in a position to report on the quality of decision making as it is going on, without waiting for the outcome
- Can look objectively at progress and performance and make comments and suggestions

Your decision coach is *not* someone who:

- Makes the decisions (you do!)
- Agrees with every thought you have to make you feel good
- Does the work needed to bring about the change (you do!)
- Is responsible for the outcome (you are!)
- Owns the results (you do!)
- Does not make decisions better than you can (you got this!)

Track Why You Rejected Options

The act of collecting information and looking for alternatives can kind of suck you in. It's easy to get off track, and it's tempting to just keep searching and searching so you can avoid deciding. We've all heard of analysis-paralysis, and it's never a good thing. One way to sidestep getting stuck in analysis is to set a time limit to the activity of doing investigation. How big or small that time limit is depends on what is important to your situation—so look to your self-knowledge and acceptance descriptions and let them guide you.

> Set a time limit for your analysis and organize how you will track your findings.

It's important you keep track of the following:

- The information and its source
- The options and your motivation for keeping or rejecting each option
- Alignment for the options with your pre-defined preferences

The tracking doesn't have to be fancy, you just need something to come back and reference when you do the next two bias-busting techniques: the Pre-Mortem and the Decision Quality Review.

A simple table will do. Here is an example:

Option	Source	Viable?	Aligns with Preferences?
Move to NE	Offer with Acme	Yes	Yes
Move to LA	Offer with Jo	No	No—I don't trust Jo; offer does not meet my $ criteria; housing is expensive; kids had negative reaction

Pre-Mortems

A Pre-Mortem is a simple thought experiment—a technique created by Gary Klein[30] that helps to identify risks associated with a decision. Here's how you do it. Right before the final decision, when you have a draft plan in hand but you haven't really started executing it yet, imagine you made the decision you have in mind, it's a year later, and the results are a *complete fail.* Now use your imagination and find as many flaws as you can; write down every reason you can think of for the failure. Finally, review the list and look for ways to strengthen the draft plan and use that going forward.

I used this technique in my own big decision making of how to treat stage-zero cervical cancer. This is described in detail in my first book, *Hypothesis, an HPV Healing Experiment.* When I decided to use yoga and naturopathic treatments to fight HPV and heal the cervical lesions, I thought, *what would a complete fail look like?* The lesions could progressively get worse and turn into actual cancer. I would then be treating cancer, and no longer healing from pre-cancer. How could I modify my experiment to avoid that happening? I involved my original gynecologist, to do the standard abnormal cell screenings and labs in between treatment rounds, about every three to five months. If the abnormal cells declined, or stayed the same, I would continue the yogic breathing and naturopathic treatment course. If the abnormal cells got worse, I would switch my approach to the originally recommended mainstream treatment for cervical lesions and have them removed surgically.

I did have to go through the additional annoyance and cost of a bunch of screenings my insurance didn't cover; however, *my confidence* in the idea that I would get the results I wanted soared! I could completely envision the healing occurring and I knew the people I would thank for that. Every time I thought about what I was doing, it felt like I was already healthy and healed. And then . . . I was!

The pre-mortem exercise is a relatively quick and simple thing to do, but if you need any more motivation to go through the energy involved in this kind of oppositional thinking, it turns out that imagining the event has already occurred increases the ability to correctly identify reasons for future outcomes by 30% (yes, 30%!)

This is an especially useful thing to do if the decision requires a team of people to do the work. It legitimizes dissent, giving people the permission to question the decision and the plan, reducing the illusion of optimism.

Decision Quality Review

By this point, you fully understand the problem you are solving, you have inventoried your own self-knowledge preferences, you have gathered information, you have reviewed options, you rejected some options and you are getting ready to select the option you plan to go into action with. As recommended by our grandfathers of cognitive bias busting, Kahneman, Lovallo, and Sibony,[31] this is your opportunity to check one final time for cognitive bias, by taking a moment for a Decision Quality Control check.

It's important that the Quality Control check is reviewed by someone *other than* the people who are making the recommendations (remember, they can't see their bias!).

Here are the three main points to cover in the Quality Review. Just go down it as a checklist.

1. Questions you, as the decision maker, should ask yourself.
    - ☑ Is anyone involved to date motivated by self-interest? (Any Scammin' Cams here?)
    - ☑ Are the people making recommendations minimizing risks and exaggerating benefits?
    - ☑ If there were contradictory recommendations, were the conflicts explored sufficiently?

2. Questions to ask about those making recommendations.
    - ☑ Were recommendations based on past success stories? If yes, the comparisons might not be valid to the current situation; be sure you understand how the comparisons to the current problem apply.
    - ☑ Have viable alternatives been offered and evaluated? There should be more than only one option.
    - ☑ Imagine you had to make this decision AGAIN, in a year. Is there more information you would want? If yes, see if you can get it now.
    - ☑ If numbers were involved, do you know where they came from and which were facts versus which were estimates? What were the estimates based on?

☑ Was the person providing the recommendation branded as 'excellent'? Does what made them great apply to your situation?

☑ Was the person providing the recommendation already heavily invested in their approach? If the previous history didn't exist, would this still be the recommendation?

3. Questions to ask about evaluating the proposed plan of action.

☑ Does it sound overly optimistic? Does it sound like they are on a 'winning streak'? (Remember that 'hot' extra roll in the game of Aggravation?)

☑ Has the plan been compared at all to similar historic plans?

☑ Has there been consideration for the effect or impact the change will have after it's realized? Are any negative reactions anticipated?

☑ Was a pre-mortem carried out? Did it prompt any changes to the recommended plan?

☑ Is the plan overly cautious? (Have you thought about what you would have your best friend do?)

Okay, so, that was quite a lot of questions; why are we doing this again? Is this a waste of time? We have already applied all the tools in our bias-busting toolbox, after all. Honestly, the time to think about these questions is pretty minimal compared to everything you are doing to ensure you make a good decision.

> The real hurdle here is *accepting* that highly experienced, very competent, well-intentioned, expert people are in the same boat we all are in when it comes to thinking and decision-making illusions.

So the quality check? Totally worth it.

61

Have a Process (and Follow It)

We already recognize the importance of collecting information before we make choices, and we know the power of applying our intuition to tough decisions, so does it matter what order we do these things?

Absolutely yes! Think first, then bring your intuition into the mix.

The problem with gathering information *after* you have already drawn a conclusion with your gut feeling is that you just can't stop yourself from gathering information that confirms your hunch. At that point, any information collection effort is just a waste of time.[32] Remember my executive sponsor who already had all the answers before I even began the analysis? Yep, that's a recipe for wasting resources, including time.

The key to making better decisions is to have all the information gathered, structured, and analyzed first. Once you can look at the information, then see how you feel about the options. This approach will help you sort out your assumptions and expectations from facts and evidence.

I picture myself singing that rhyme like I did when I was a kid, before jumping off the swing (don't tell my mom!): One for the money, two for the show, three to get ready and four to GO! I couldn't just skip the money, the show, and the getting ready part; those were very important, allowing me to reach maximum swing height so when I let go I was fully committed to soaring as far as possible.

(one for the money)	Gather information and perform analysis.
(two for the show)	Overlay calm, clear wisdom.
(three to get ready)	Choose the best option.
(and four to GO!)	Move forward toward the results.

If the song isn't something that works for you, here is the shorter mantra version: **Think-Feel-Choose-Act.**

This is a general thinking process, so you will find yourself doing it over and over again as you make the series of decisions needed to design a plan and then perform all the actions necessary to bring about change.

Think-Feel-Choose-Act

1. Perform analysis
2. Apply intuition
3. Choose your direction
4. Act with the end in mind

Bias-Busting Toolkit Inventory

☑ Trust-Me Notebook

☑ A Space to Breathe

☑ Curious Attitude

☑ Self-Knowledge Baseline
  ★ Knowledge of Problem
  ★ Friends with Fear
  ★ Values and Beliefs Based on Joy
  ★ Success Criteria
  ★ Acceptance of Current Situation
  ★ Perspective of What You'd Have Your Best Friend Do

☑ Decision Coach

☑ Track Rejected Options and Reasoning

☑ Pre-mortem

☑ Decision Quality Review

☑ Decision Making Process
  ★ Think first *then* Feel: Think-Feel-Choose-Act
  ★ 3 Step Choice Making
      Step 1 Choose You
      Step 2 Choose Action
      Step 3 Choose Change

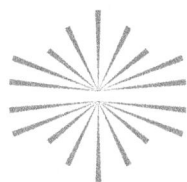

CHAPTER · 4

THREE DECISION MAKING
STRATEGIES THAT REALLY WORK

WHY FOLLOW A PROCESS?

Many experts consider courage to be a key ingredient for decision making. Specifically, the courage that comes from confidence in the decision-making process.[33] Often times, people struggle with making difficult decisions because they don't have a methodology to follow, and that results in low confidence in their ability to make tough decisions. It's even more than a cognitive illusion working against us, it's the brain itself working against us!

When we face change, we face uncertainty. As it turns out, uncertainty affects the brain since it's wired to react to uncertainty with fear.[34] The rational, thinking part of the brain yields control to the limbic system where emotions are generated. When that happens, we are more prone to irrational and erratic decisions. What we need to do is re-engage our rational thinking to keep us on track.

The way to do that is to have a decision-making process.

[When people face change,] They know that the only thing they really control is the process through which they reach their decisions. That's the only rational way to handle the unknown, and the best way to keep your head on level ground.

Dr. Travis Bradberry,
cofounder of TalentSmart

The simple process I created will guide you through the uncertainty and land you in a position of readiness for change.

Here is the model we have been working with so far:

Choice-making system

Focus: aspects of intuition to include in decision making:

Joy, Acceptance, Trust, Thankfulness.

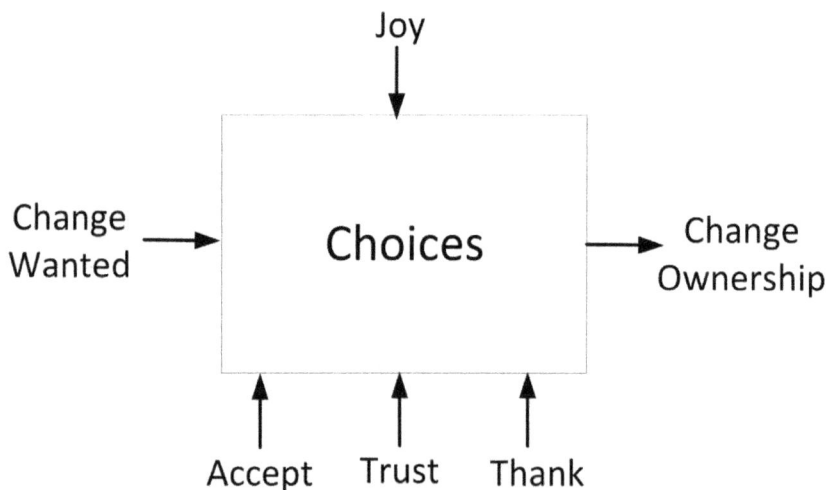

Joy
↓

Change Wanted → | **Choices** | → Change Ownership

↑ ↑ ↑
Accept Trust Thank

Now we are going to drill into it, so the focus is on what we need to do to transform the input (the change you want) into the output (the change when you have it and own it).

THREE-STEP CHOICE-MAKING PROCESS

Here's what we need to do to transform desired change into achieved change.

1. Choose You
2. Choose Action
3. Choose Change

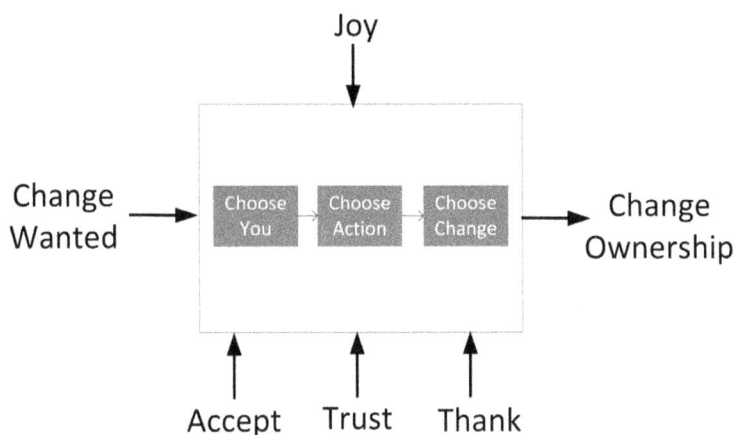

Courage in decision-making comes from confidence; confidence comes from the process you use to make the decision.

Beth Harper, President of
Clinical Performance Partners, Inc.[35]

STEP 1: CHOOSE YOU

Overview Step 1: Choose You
In this step you will
☑ Revisit your self-knowledge baseline
☑ Align it with your personal Joy story

By now it should be no surprise to you that the first step in the choice-making process is to know your preferences; yes, it's not by chance that it's the same thing we learned to do to in order to neutralize cognitive illusions in decision making.

Here's a quick review of what you defined when establishing your self-knowledge baseline.

1. Your problem.
2. Your values and beliefs.
3. Your vision of success.
4. Your acceptance of the current situation.

If you played along with this exercise in building your Bias-Busting toolbox, you have these written down already! Now is a good time to pull out that Trust-Me notebook and look over your entries.

Along with the self-knowledge baseline, it's time to add *the feeling* that will motivate you to keep moving forward. A great approach is to have an inspiring theme; you can think of it as naming your *north star.* This star must be bright enough to align everyone involved with *your* preferences.

Sometimes organizations might call a theme like this their corporate story,[36] mission, or credo. I like to simply call it your Joy.

It's important to note the *position* of your Joy in the decision-making process. If you look at where it is in the choice-making framework, it's at the top, in *the* position of influence over everything in the system of procedures.

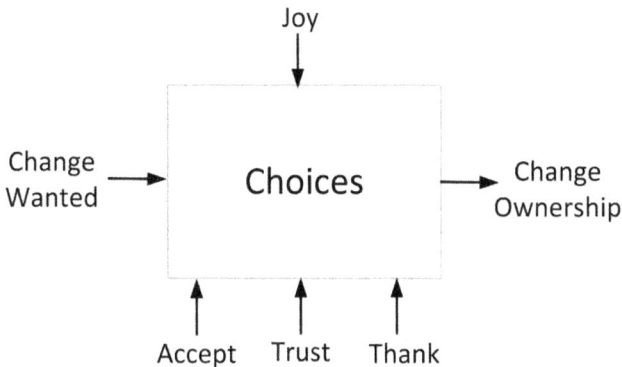

Joy
↓

Change
Wanted → **Choices** → Change
Ownership

↑ ↑ ↑
Accept Trust Thank

There is another way to look at this same system: in this view, put your north star in the middle.

71

Joy-centered Decision Process

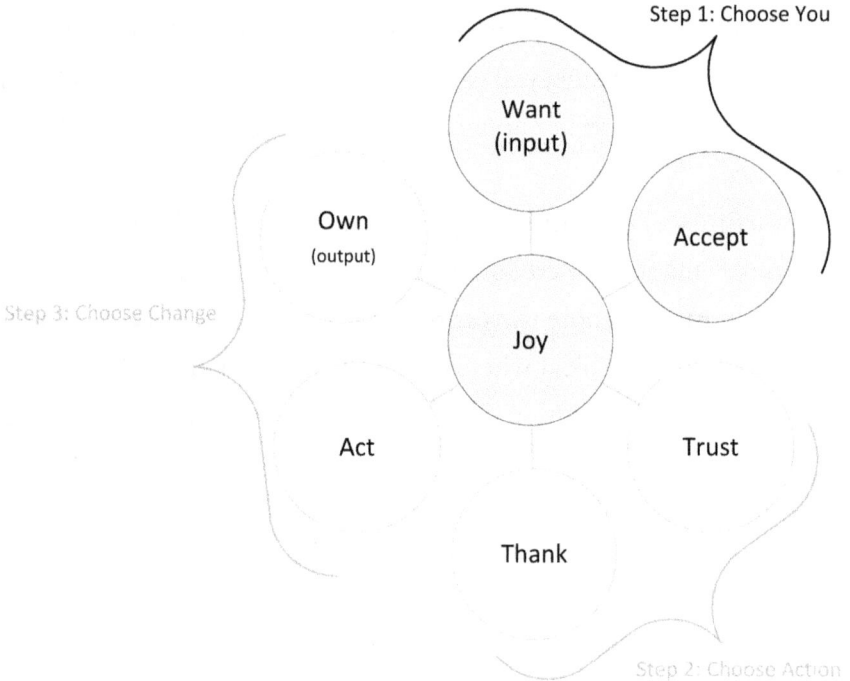

Either depiction is correct—just pick the model that works with your way of thinking. I am offering this to you because adopting this process should be from a position of freedom—choice (not chore!).

With this circular model, you can envision entering the process at the top starting with defining what you want, and then go around clockwise, until you end up owning the result. The diagram identifies the parts of the decision process that apply to each of the three steps. At all times, Joy is in the middle connecting the dots.

Joy is in the middle
connecting the dots of your steps
that bring about change.

Influenced by Scientific Method

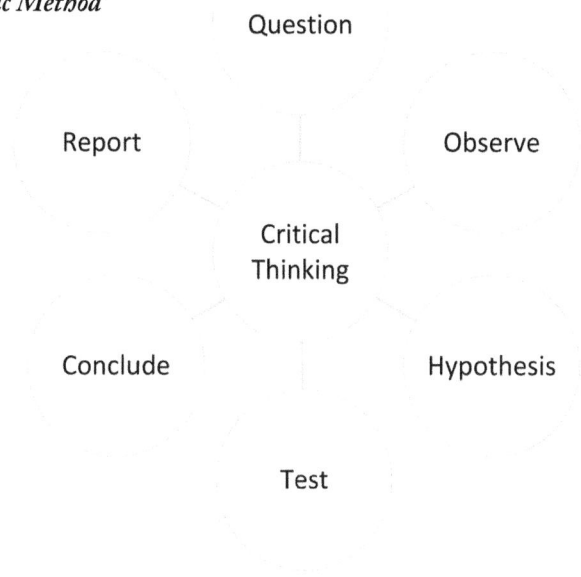

To placate your curiosity (I know you are wondering!), I want to share the back story to this process. You already know I created it by documenting how I went through my own HPV healing experiment. But how did I know what steps to take in that very first experiment? Well, I can't get around the irony that I applied *the scientific method* to test my body's response to healing methods often considered to be founded on pseudoscience. So yes, this process is heavily influenced by the scientific method. Do you see it?

Scientific Method

Question

Report   Observe

Critical
Thinking

Conclude   Hypothesis

Test

It's easy to understand how *critical thinking connects the dots* of the scientific method. Can you imagine what kind of results a scientist might get if somewhere in the experiment the scientist stopped thinking critically? The whole thing would just fall apart!

So in our choice-making process, joy connects the dots. If you go just a little deeper, and overlay these two models, critical thinking and joy have an interesting relationship. Remember in the first chapter when we considered what *motivates* thinking? We discovered the attitudes of Prairie Chicken Pippen, Scammin' Cam, Wise Winn. This model again suggests an important element of critical thinking is having the 'right' attitude. I am suggesting the 'right' attitude is founded in Joy.

> An important element of critical thinking is to have the right attitude, and if you listen to your inner wisdom, that right attitude is founded in Joy.

It's important to make the commitment to place your joy in the middle of your decisions and actions. If Joy is left out to bounce around in only the areas where you feel comfortable, or Joy is there only when you have time for it—the likelihood of getting the results you are hoping for is reduced.

Joy and Story Telling

Putting words to your north star (or to the central thing that connects all the dots) is an exercise in articulating what makes you feel alive, and that is *not* easy! Just saying out loud what you really want is deceptively difficult; but saying what your joy is, that's pretty much level-10 communication, even when just talking to yourself!

So don't press it. Just go to your space to breathe, and begin to tell a story, *your* story. What story will you tell yourself inside your head to encourage you along this journey of bringing about change? Here's a suggestion: tell the story that makes you smile and sigh and feel, Yeah, that's right, that's me, that's what I stand for.

Stories are not only a powerful way to connect people, but also a powerful way to connect you with your inner truth. How do you know when you are on the right track? Your story will bring you to that moment quickly. Your story will allow you to experience all those factoids and bits and all the changes and choices you are now facing in a holistic way. Your story will inspire you and can be used to increase your commitment. Your story can even be used to remove obstacles.

Finding Your Joy Story—It's Not Always What You Think

I have a friend who shared with me a great example of someone who has found his Joy. He was a previous co-worker, and we get together every now and then to catch up on things. The last time I met him, as soon as we hugged hello, he immediately pulled out his phone to share his story.

Friend: (still riding the bliss wave, he could hardly contain himself) I have to show you this video. You know that raft I bought last year? Well I got one of those GoPros and strapped it to my helmet, and check this out! See that, yeah, every person in the raft in front of us was in the water. Then we all had to do a mini-rescue mission. With only one raft, several had to wait for us to come back and get them with the car. I stayed with the hurt guy. He was fine, just a little sore and shaken up. Do you believe that? I love that raft. I love being on the water.

Me: Wow, that's incredible. So, do you have more video of everyone still *in* the boat? You know, the actual rafting part?

Friend: No, not really, this happened just like minutes after we were a bit down river from the place where we put in.

Me: Oh my, so you only rafted just a few minutes and then helped the others the whole *rest* of your rafting day?

Friend: (chuckling to himself) Yeah, it was still great. Rafting, all of it, it just makes me feel really alive. You know? I will take it any way I can get it!

Me: (to myself) Hey, I'm not judging what other people consider an 'alive' moment, but OMG does that sound like a crap day to me! And yet . . . there is no denying that smile I see on his face, the sparkle in his eye and the excitement in his voice.

To us on the outside, it's not obvious what my friend's joy really is. Is it rafting? Is it rescuing, or the opportunity of rescuing? Is it the slight sense of danger? The fun of never really knowing what's going to happen? All those nuances are wrapped up in the joy of rafting. This joy is something he prioritizes and invests in. This is what he comes back to, time and time again, to refresh and re-energize.

What's Your Joy Story?

- A key point here is to be authentic.
- Ask yourself, when you are facing a tough decision, what is your guiding light?
- This is clearly not about what brings your friends Joy.
- Not what your mom thinks brings Joy.
- It's certainly not what social media is currently selling as Joy.

You can only find your Joy by looking within you.

There is probably no hard data on what makes you feel alive. More likely than not, your joy story is different than it was, say, ten years ago, or even one year ago, or even yesterday before you knew about this problem you have to solve.

Bottom line: it's important to give yourself the permission to define *your* joy, and it's okay if it's a story you've never had before. When you take time to look, what you find might surprise you, in a good way!

> At the core, your joy story will tell the tale of self-acceptance and self-love.

The great part is you don't have to change anything, it's already there inside you. It doesn't matter if what makes you feel alive sounds unusual or something others may think is on the fringe of social acceptance. It's about defining what matters to you and having it in your life. The more you can feel it every day, the better; it will compel you to adopt the new habits and activities coming your way. It is important to continue feeling joy while you are going through all this. Your Joy will be the catalyst for your actions.

Write down, right now, here or in your Trust-Me notebook, a few notes about Your Joy Story.

🖋 My Joy Story

Want a couple examples?

Think of corporate stories that have really resonated with you and use that as a model for making your own personal story. Most everyone is familiar with the slogan "Just Do It" from Nike. It's easy to understand how that slogan can not only motivate customers, but also align and motivate their own staff to move into action and make those decisions needed to bring products to market.

My personal Joy story from my book *Hypothesis: an HPV Experiment* sounded like this: I will have my whole cervix and my whole sex life. I will talk openly with those I love about what I am going through. I will be true to my inner voice. I will share my experience to help reduce the stigmas and grow awareness around HPV, sex, age, alternative medicine and alternative lifestyles.

I know, not as elegant as Nike's story; but it's all *my* story, and it aligned myself and everyone who helped me reach my goal to heal from HPV and cervical lesions.

Now of course my whole life's story is not about healing HPV! But it was my story for that particular problem and need to bring change in my life. So it might be helpful to know you don't have to define your *life* story, just the story about the change you are currently wanting to bring into your life.

Wrap Joy into Your Preferences

Now it's time to connect the dots between what you want and what you accept about your current situation with your Joy.

Here's the action: while you revisit your self-knowledge baseline, overlay them with your Joy story.

> Revisit your self-knowledge baseline and overlay them with what brings you Joy.

It will look something like this.

1. Know the problem, and *how it's decreasing or prohibiting your Joy.*
2. Know your values and beliefs, *and what brings you Joy.*
3. Know what success looks like, *and how it increases your Joy.*
4. Accept where you are now, *and embrace what brings you Joy.*

What you are doing is layering your gut feelings and attitude onto some solid information you have gathered about your problem and current situation.

The idea of intuition helping you commit to decisions is even supported by some recent studies out of the Universities of Toronto Scarborough and Yale.[38] Two groups were asked to make the same decision, but one group was encouraged to decide using their intuition, and the other was encouraged to base their decision on logic.

Participants who were encouraged to use their intuition more frequently agreed *the decision reflected their true selves* and then showed they were *greater advocates for their decision by sharing it with more friends* than the logic-based group did. Just by feeling the decision reflected their values, it affected their actual behavior!

And that's exactly what you accomplish with Step 1: Choosing You.

Step 2: Choose Action

Overview Step 2: Choose Action
In this step you will
☑ Apply three qualities of trust in evaluating options
☑ Make a plan that includes measurements and communication
☑ Perform a choice-making quality review

Time to Trust

You have done the work in knowing what you want and accepting accountability. As much effort as that was, frankly you are now at what is most likely the hardest step in the process. What's so hard? Well, now, it's time to trust.

Because you are working through a tough decision, chances are you don't know *how* to get yourself through to the end or you don't have the skill or capability to do all the things that need to be done. You are in a position of having to trust the advice and actions of other people. You are asking for help.

Emotionally, you are exposing your vulnerability to others. In your search for information and advice, you need to believe the people you

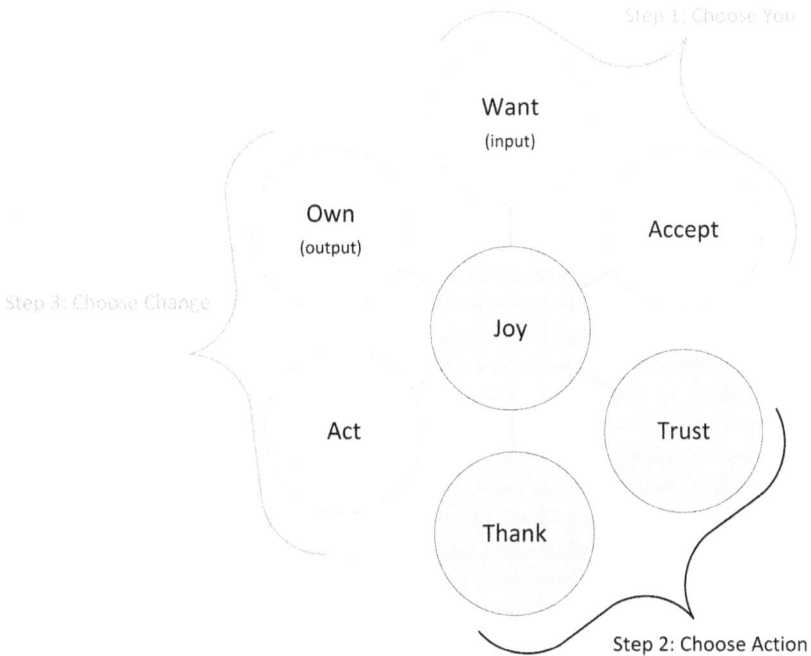

reach out to will not take advantage of the position you are in. The actions you take involve depending on your advisors and providers to come through and deliver on what they say. So clearly, trust is what you need to offer up at this point.

Don't get me wrong: this is not necessarily the time to trust *more*, because trust is differentiated.

> *Have more trust in the trustworthy, but not in the untrustworthy.*
>
> Onora O'Neill, Member of Parliament
> of the United Kingdom[38]

Trust is a perfect example of the pairing of thinking and feeling, since trust is both an emotion and a logical action. Here's where shifting your brain first into thinking mode is going to help you make good choices. *Remember: Think-Feel-Choose-Act.* When reviewing advice, consider these three things for each option:

1. Are they honest?
2. Are they competent?
3. Are they reliable?

The people who you are taking advice from, including your decision coach, must provide adequate evidence they are trustworthy. If it makes sense, you can add this to your option tracker.

Here is the simple tracker example from our Bias-Busting toolkit.

OPTION	SOURCE	VIABLE?	ALIGNS WITH PREFERENCES
Move to NE	Offer with Acme	Yes	Yes
Move to LA	Offer with Jo	No	No—I don't trust Jo,; offer does not meet my $ criteria; housing is expensive; spouse had negative reaction

What this allows us to do is be a little more specific about what 'viable' means. Part of being a viable option is that the people associated with the option are trustworthy.

Option	Honest	Competent	Reliable	Preferences & Joy Align	Keep or Reject
Acme in NE	Yes	Yes	Yes	Yes	Go forward
Jo's Co in LA	Yes	Yes	No	No—$ No— spouse	Reject: Spouse not onboard

In this case we know the reason I don't trust Jo is because, though he is honest, and competent, based on what he has shared with me, I don't think he will be reliable. And so he gets a 'no' rating on trustworthiness.

From what we have covered so far, we are tracking the following for each option:

1. Are the people involved in this option trustworthy?
   - Purpose: move forward in change I can't do all by myself.
2. Does this option align with my preferences?
   - Purpose: protect myself from people using my cognitive illusions for their gain (not so much mine).
3. Does this option align with my Joy story?
   - Purpose: Motivation and inspiration.
4. Why am I rejecting this option?
   - Purpose: Track reasoning for quality review and to gain confidence in my intuition going forward.

The bonus you maybe didn't see coming . . .

Once you've made this choice, and select who you will trust, you are in an amazingly powerful position: you can fully put the problem into their capable hands and *shift your full focus* on visualizing the results.

> Once you decide who and what you are going to trust, direct all your energy towards visualizing the results.

You can start letting yourself feel the relief of knowing the problem is over. Of course, it's not yet in physical life—you haven't started the work yet! That said, it's to your advantage to begin letting your heart feel like it's already at the goal line.

Do you remember a time you allowed yourself to trust? How did it feel? How did it affect your ability to realize the change you wanted? I still remember the moment I chose to trust my yoga teacher and the complementary treatment option of breathing and moving as part of my strategy to heal from HPV.

"The notion of alternative medicine just wasn't something I ever seriously considered. And though I have grown to trust my teacher and her expertise in this area, breathing as an approach to address illness honestly sounded pretty over-the-top hippy for me. We arranged for me to come to the next week's class where she would introduce me to some pranayama, which is Sanskrit for "breath control", where prana means "life force". There was a cold wind to fight as I went to my car after that. I was twirling all this in my mind.

As I reflected on her suggestion that yogic breathing practices could help me, *I felt this huge sigh of relief* (yep, a deep-to-the soul-exhale, it was like that). *A warm wave of hope came over me.* Her notion of breathing to heal immediately felt like something I wanted. It resonated with me. *I knew this was something I could hold onto.*"[39]

Trust Yourself

To be able to make choices, there is no getting around the fact that the first person you have to trust is yourself. Have you found yourself in the same position as my customer support friend, mentioned in the foreword: the position where you just don't trust yourself to make tough decisions?

It's my hope that you will find something you can hold onto in this Choice-Making Process. By having a simple method to follow, you may experience a sense of relief and be in a position to deepen trust in your inner voice. With just a few tools you can begin putting the problem behind you and begin forming a vision of having the results as soon as possible.

Gain trust in your choice making ability because we make hard choices all the time.

Ruth Chang, American
professor of philosophy[40]

Make the Damn Plan

Even if your trusted helpers are describing for you what specific actions need to occur, you will still want to make your own plan of action. It doesn't have to be complicated.

At a minimum, your plan of action should include:
1. Start time
2. Significant tasks, events, or milestones
3. Activities that reflect your Joy story
4. Thank-you moments
5. Measurement: when and how progress is visible
6. Communication: your preferences, your plan, your progress, your course corrections
7. Results indicator

You may be asking yourself, really, do I need to go through all that? I already made my big choice and now there's more? Well yes, that big choice was just the beginning—now is the action part!

Having a simple plan is useful for many things, like getting your mind in the right place to take action. That said, I would argue that the most important reason to have a plan is to enable course correction.

Have a plan to inform and manage course correction.

Here is an example of a challenging choice I made that needed a plan: My plan for going alone to a nightclub for the first time.

Some of you may be thinking, seriously, you need a plan for that? What I can tell you is what people think is a tough decision varies wildly. And for me, newly divorced after over 20 years of marriage, yes, just getting out of my own living room was a thing, and going to a nightclub alone was a *big* thing.

Back story: My ex-husband and I had a custom of when we went out to a bar and saw a military member in uniform there, we would occasionally buy drinks or dessert for them as a random 'thank you for your service' moment. We had been divorced for a couple of years, and I genuinely missed doing this. I felt I avoided bars and dance places for long enough.

So what was the big decision? I *decided it was time* to do a little personal growth and learn how to go it alone to nightclubs. In Portland there is an annual event called "Fleet Week". This is where military ships come in to celebrate the annual Rose Festival with us. It gives the citizens a chance to see and tour ships and honor military members. It gives military members an opportunity for a fun break. I was excited about this because this year, I could use that as an opportunity to get over my nightclub aversion. I was determined to find out where the sailors were likely to go and buy them drinks.

It turned out the universe heard me, and presented a flyer on the street I frequented during my lunch hour walk. "Military Members Entrance Free" it said. Music, dance floor, buffet and full bar. I knew *that* was the place to play out my decision.

Excited me: Who knows who I might meet?

Fearful me: What did I decide? Am I crazy? A nightclub alone? Isn't that supposed to be dangerous?

Inner-voice encouragement me: You got this, Terrie. It's your town, you know what you want, you are not going to get talked into anything. Go have an adventure! Calm down, create a plan and do this thing!

Terrie's Plan to go to a nightclub alone

1. **Start time:** I had desire for change, the flyer presented an opportunity. Perfect! Free Day for Sailors is June 6. I have eight days to learn about this place and get my act together.

2. **Significant tasks:** Learn about this place, vibe, hours, etc. Contact my son to be my safety partner, who knows where I am and when, and is available for bailout calls if needed. Get my nails done. Make sure my dress still fits. Make sure my bank account can handle the tab. Leave once my results are achieved.

3. **Activities that make me feel alive:** Listening to people's stories, music and dancing. Self-knowledge note: "no dancing" was not an option; this turned out useful in narrowing possible location choices.

4. **Thank you moment:** Take my son to lunch this week. Easy, that was a Joy activity too.

5. **Measurement:** Checklist that all the above are available. Do the place research first, in case you have to find a different place. Do the dress thing more sooner than later in case I have to buy clothes.

6. **Communication:** Give final go-ahead to my son the day before the event and when I get back home.

7. **Results indicator:** I get over the bar-alone fear, I thank sailors for their contribution to my country and bought drinks.

Hopefully you are thinking, well that kind of planning comes pretty natural. Yes, planning is natural for a lot of us. If it is for you, use that to your advantage. Just acknowledging you *have* a plan, and then the bonus of writing your plan down in your Trust-Me notebook, you are more likely to commit to seeing it through. Here's what happened and how my plan helped me. It starts when something unexpected arises.

Hurdle #1: While gathering information to get to my first milestone, I learned the night club was a *sex club*.

Stunned me: A sex club? Huh. So, those are real.

Runaway from the unfamiliar me: Nope, bail on it. This is about buying sailors drinks, not about sexing them.

Curious me: (and the curiosity thing *always* gets me!) I wonder what a sex club is anyway? Dang, now I can't stop wondering! Look, they have an online forum to ask questions every night at 7 . . .

Course correction #1: Add thirty minutes of online question/answer time for the next three nights with the various moderators and see if this place is still a go. I learned a lot of things in that online forum! But a key point that pertained to my immediate goals and plan was learning that the parking was tricky and potentially by a not-safe street.

Course correction #2: Make a drive-by a day in advance to figure out the streets that get into the safer parking. Have a staff member walk me to my car.

I learned that I needed time for them to run a security check over my ID, plus time to fill out release forms. Also there was a tour offered the first thirty minutes after doors opening.

Course correction #3: Go early, before the club gets busy, not 'fashionably late club style' like one of my friends suggested. The tour will provide an additional view into this place and a chance for me to consider if I want to leave before things even get started.

In the end, I spent more time on prep activities than I thought I would, but it was worth it. I was informed, my safety person was informed, I was confident and not worried. I met at least six people who didn't seem that different from me via the online forum and some of them were going to be there that night. Going it alone got quite a bit less lonely.

> The point is, with a plan in hand, I didn't follow to my 'bail now' emotion, I kept moving forward toward my big decision.

I had a great time, by the way, and achieved all the results I was going for, plus bonuses! I bought many sailors drinks and watched many of them dance in the go-go cage with a woman in a lace onesie celebrating her seventieth birthday. She quickly became a new hero of mine! I heard many people's stories. I enjoyed the music and danced (even next to some naked dancers). The security staff were well trained; I never felt threatened or unsafe. I can honestly say it was an eye-opening and life-changing event to see that challenging decision through.

Bottom line, make the damn plan; it will give you confidence to move forward (remember, there is no wrong decision really). The plan makes course correction easier to understand and manage.

The Importance of Measurement

Always, always have a way to measure the progress on your decision. Again, it doesn't have to be complicated, just something to keep your thinking engaged so your feeling side doesn't throw you off track.

Remember your self-knowledge baseline, and when you defined up front what success would look like for you? Measure your progress towards what you specifically outlined as success. Monitoring measurements will give you confidence you are on your way to realizing that.

Examples of measurement check-ins:

- I am at day three of eight, are a reasonable amount of my activities accomplished?
- I had lab work done to see if my bio-readings are changing, are the intermittent screenings showing the progression I am expecting?
- I have spent this much of my budgeted dollars, it that reasonable for where I am in the process?

- I have a sales cycle coming up in two months, is the product offering ready for pre-sales communication?

It's a good idea to consider when in your plan are measurement check-ins most effective. Just like having a plan, the key point in progress measurement is this allows you to see where things are, so you can course correct *when* it is needed. You don't want to check when it's too late to do anything about an undesirable measurement finding.

> *The ability to make the right choice when it really matters is a skill that will serve you well for the entirety of your adult life.*
>
> Steven Johnson, author of *Farsighted*[41]

Communicate, Communicate, Communicate

Times of measurement check-ins are also a good time to reach out and communicate with others that are involved in your plan. That way you can keep everyone updated with any course-correction decisions you've made, so everyone continues to be aligned and working the plan according to your preferences.

This is also a good time to communicate Thank You.

Thank You

If expressing gratitude isn't already on your list of activities that make you feel alive, we got it covered: thank-you moments are explicitly mentioned as an essential activity in your plan of action. Thinking, feeling and doing gratitude will fuel your passion for continuing to move forward in your plan.

You don't have to wait for something wonderful to happen to be thankful for it. As part of your plan, describe who you will thank and how you will thank them.

The Gift

I've learned from various business practices that incorporating thank-you gifts into the deal or the project was essential. When I was brokering real estate, it was the "closing gift". I loved giving my clients a nice rose bush for their new property. From a sales thinking point of view, it helped me to "know" in at least this one simple way that the deal would actually close—it seemed natural that would be how things concluded. I never really thought much about not being able to close—I have the rose planned, after all! And besides that, it just felt good old-fashioned nice. When that bush bloomed all summer like it does here in Oregon, I imagined them telling their neighbors a little about me and how I helped them find their new home.

When I was a technical project manager, we always budgeted for a team project close celebration and a memento for each team member that reminded them of their contribution to a successful project. Staff members who had been part of many projects would have a little lineup of cute mementos as a proud display on their desks. Again, from a project manager perspective, this was great for my personal head game: I never really thought that the project wouldn't finish, they always finish. And I never really thought that there wouldn't be something to celebrate in the end—there always was something that went to market. I mean, we bought the project desk toy, after all! And then, in the end, this simple token bonded us in a small way.

I will be honest, having a vision of gratitude and planning actual thank-you moments is ultimately somewhat selfish. The real gift is the one you give yourself. For me, I need to manage the head game. I need something tangible to combat doubt. I need to really believe I can have this thing I am planning on having. What is the gift you will give yourself?

> *There's a growing body of research on the benefits of gratitude. Studies have found that giving thanks and counting blessings can help people sleep better, lower stress and improve interpersonal relationships.*
>
> Clinical Psychology Review article[42]

How to Win Over the Head (and Heart)

Create a vision of gratitude right away and *as a daily task*, begin feeling thankful for having what you want.

My visions of gratitude occur as part of my morning meditation. It didn't take long to notice that the undeniably joyful feeling this brings me is, frankly, slightly addictive. I noticed that the intention behind my wanting to extend thanks wasn't like other moments of saying thank you that I'd had before, like in real estate and project management: it isn't to differentiate myself amongst others. It's not about demonstrating my creativity or uniqueness. It's not to spotlight one of my thank-ees over the other. It's not to grow my 'account' with anyone. It's not about retaining these people as my friends. These precious gratitude moments I have in meditation help me to believe I will receive the results I am working toward. After a while, feeling gratitude starts to *equate* to the feeling of what it's like to have the desired results. It's like opening your Christmas presents early.

How to Create a Vision of Gratitude

Transform all the results you are expecting into tangible actions of gratitude. Visualize attaining your results like it's already happened to you. Who will you thank? How will you thank them? Visualize every aspect of the thank-you moment. Picture everything: how you feel, the lighting, temperature and sounds, etc.

What physical tokens or symbols of personal connection would you like to give? What do you need to prepare? Do you need to make any arrangements for them to be able to receive this?

Then, put the thank-you activities on your action plan.

There Is No Wrong Way to Say Thank You

When I was a kid, I delivered a thank you incorrectly. I was with my grandma, and we visited one of her friends. As we were on our way out the door, I forgot to say thank you. So in the car, my grandma scolded me, and told me to march right back up there to the door and say thank you. I was horrified on a couple levels. I was embarrassed I forgot the manners my mom painstakingly taught me. I felt terrible.

I managed to do something that made my grandma scold me—she never got mad at me! I was asked to bring further attention to all this by doing the walk of shame back to the door of my grandma's friend. How do you do a Sorry and a Thank You at the same time anyway? Being what it was, I slinked back up to her door, which she was still standing in, and said, "My grandma told me to thank you." This choice to not deliver gratitude with my own intent of appreciation earned me a swat and an ear-pulling back to the car. I think it was ever since that time, I have always been a bit fearful of expressing gratitude. Clearly, saying thank you the wrong way could get you into big trouble.

As it turns out, all that 'big trouble' stuff—I let go of all that, because

I am very sure that if you expect nothing in return, and your intent is your own, there is no wrong way to say thank you.

Wherever they are, if they've loved you and encouraged you and wanted what was best in life for you, they're right inside yourself. And I feel that you deserve quiet time on this special occasion to devote some thought to them, so let's just take a minute in honor of those who have cared about us all along the way.

Fred McFeely Rogers[43]

With an action plan in hand, it's the perfect time to run through the following choice-making quality review. This checklist will ensure we have done the best we can to think first in order to avoid those pesky cognitive illusions. It will also help ensure we have done the best we can to weave in the power of our inner wisdom and intuition. Just go down the list, and if there was anything missed, now is the time to tend to that gap before moving forward with full confidence in your decision to bring about change.

Ten-Point Choice Quality Review

1. Step 1: Choose Me

   ☑ I understand the problem and I feel the result will address it.

   ☑ I feel my preferences are addressed in the solution option.

      ☑ I know what success looks like, and I feel confident my choices will get me there.

      ☑ The option I selected aligns with what I value and believe.

      ☑ I accept my current situation and believe the actions I plan to take will move me forward to the change I desire.

   ☑ I validated the assumptions I made.

   ☑ I understand the source(s) of the information I gathered.

   ☑ I considered many options.

2. Step 2: Choose Action

   ☑ I feel my solution providers are trustworthy.

   ☑ I understand the impact and risks of my choice.

   ☑ As I move forward toward my desired results:

      ☑ I measure progress, so I can course correct as needed.

      ☑ I know who I will communicate progress and changes with.

      ☑ I made space for activities that make me feel alive.

      ☑ My plan includes tangible acts of gratitude.

3. Step 3: Choose Change

   ☑ I know what the care and feeding of the results entail.

   ☑ I look forward to what I will do to 'pay it forward' once the results are realized.

Step 3: Choose Change

Overview Step 3: Choose Change
In this step you will
☑ Follow your plan
☑ Journal measurements, course corrections, discoveries and results
☑ Prepare for 'care and feeding' of the outcome
☑ Pay it forward

So here we are, the final step, and this is one is a lulu.

You have done all the talk; now it's time to walk. This is the expression of commitment that really matters. All those choices you made so far are in your head and in your conversation; now they are going to be expressed in your body, by your doing.

Maybe you are thinking, What if I choose to do nothing?

Frankly, that can be a perfectly sound choice, and now is a good time to make that choice before you have invested the resources needed to go into action.

Ten-Point Choice Quality Review is done after the plan is made and before the action starts. As you looked your findings to date, did it become clear to you whether this is still a change or accomplishment

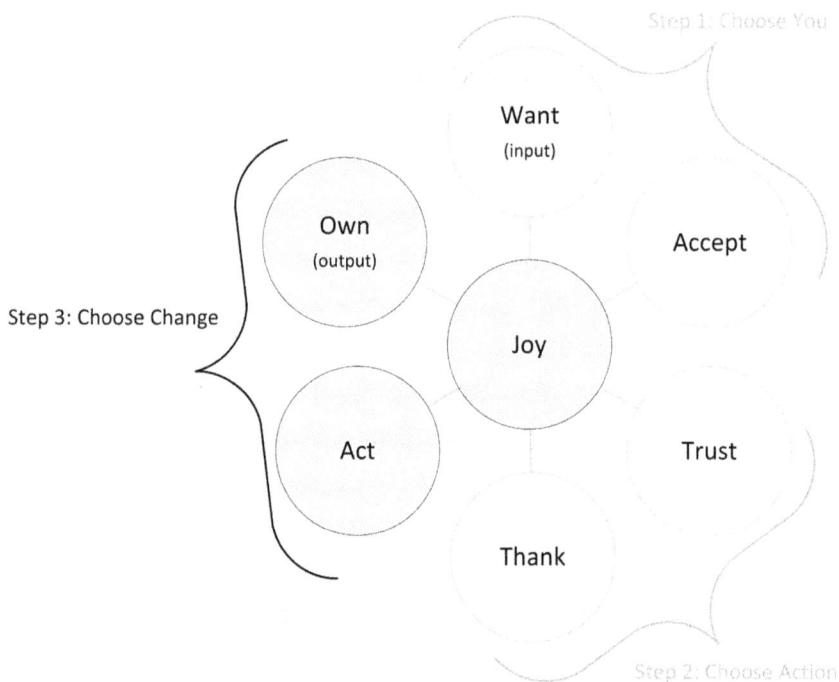

worth doing? The problem worth solving? The trust worth extending? The vision worth being thankful for?

As my yoga teacher would say: "You can do, do differently, or not do." So at this time you can move forward into action, modify your plan or any item on the Quality Review, or simply call it done at this point and chose to do nothing. All of these are good decisions.

You can do, do differently, or not do.

Britt B Steele, yoga teacher and truth seeker

98

I Choose Change

My advice at this point? Enjoy the ride, and journal it too.

The journal is primarily for savoring the moments: a memento to share with others and yourself. You can look back on it to remember how amazing it is to see yourself in action, doing the work to bring about change, accomplishments, and transformation. Capture your days in any way you like—photos, video, writing—heck, some of my best journaling is on sticky notes or by saving small tokens from events in a special container. And it doesn't just have to be the happy, beautiful, joy stuff; consider how you may want to remember the struggles, the *aha* moments, the mistakes, the people and things you are thankful for. Take it all in.

Notebook Items

There are some key things you will want to explicitly put in your Trust-Me notebook that will help you to build confidence (and speed!) in future decision making:

1. Measurements
2. Course corrections
3. Discoveries
4. Results

When you capture these, first get the objective facts, then make comments on how you feel about those things. That alone will likely raise more *aha* moments for you!

About Course Corrections

If you find out during one of your milestones that things are shifting away from your original goals, don't let that throw you off. You got this! Go back to your **Choose You** findings and create activities that put things back in alignment with your North Star—your Joy Story. If you find out your plan is no longer serving you as it was originally sketched out, for example you are not meeting your target dates, no worries! You got this! Go back to the **Choose Action** findings and change the plan to serve you.

In my HPV Healing Experiment, my original plan was to achieve the results I wanted in five months. As it turned out, my treatment plan changed three times and my timeline extended out to over a couple years. This was okay because I was still within the boundaries of my preferences and healing measurement guidelines. My timeline quadrupled because my healing progression was slow, but it was consistent and showed incremental improvement. This is a complete success *and* nothing like what I originally expected.

How Will You Own the Outcome?

Have you thought yet about what day-to-day life is going to be like once you are the proud owner of this new outcome you are bringing into the world?

Well sure, you have to some degree; but now while you are doing the work to make it real, consider what is needed to nurture and grow the result.

Take, for example, when I wanted to remodel my property. I wanted to offer a place for traveling nurses to stay while on contract with one of the many medical facilities nearby. I had passion around this idea because my family interacted almost daily with medical professionals—my brother was a brain injury patient for decades before he died.

I had property that was largely unused in an area that could make a perfect temporary home for hard-working people. The motivator? It just *felt right* to honor medical professionals in this way while still building my own financial stability. Win-win all around.

So I knew the remodel was a big project in itself, but the truly important thinking was around what it would be like to have people continuously renting and using this new space. There would be additional house maintenance, yard maintenance, cleaning in between guest stays, insurance, taxes, business license, marketing so people knew this was available. Was I ready to take on all of that? Was that sustainable? You see, I knew if I brought about this change, I couldn't just dust off the construction dust and be 'done'.

Most big decisions that bring about big change are going to bring some kind of 'new' ownership into your life. *Before* you have it is the best time to think about what all that entails! Sure, you can't predict everything. But ask yourself if there is anything you have to have in place immediately following the moment when you have the outcome you are expecting.

Ask yourself the following: What's involved in the care and feeding of this new thing I am bringing into the world?

Do you need some time off for an adjustment period? Or resources for a celebration? Do you need any special equipment you have never had around before? Do you need a new network of people to support you? Is this something that requires continuous improvement?

Taking full accountability and ownership of the results will help you in several ways.

1. You will not have regret and you won't be tempted to blame anyone for how this all turns out.

2. You will reinforce your vision of gratitude and feelings of already having what you are currently working toward.

3. You can course correct or modify your plan of action as needed for something you didn't already consider or plan for.

PAY IT FORWARD—OWN YOUR NEW WISDOM

Once you have reached the end of the plan, and you are witnessing real-life indicators of the outcome made reality, this experience is part of you. You are transformed! You are now squarely into the new life as usual, doing the everyday care and feeding of the very thing you made happen. You now have wisdom! And evidence of your hard-earned wisdom is in your journal and in your Trust-Me notebook.

What will you do with your discoveries and lessons learned?

For one thing, you can use them going forward as reference as you face more big decisions in your future, so that is all for you.

If you haven't already included the idea of Paying It Forward in your vision of gratitude, I suggest you include that now as part of owning the outcome of your decisions this far: own your wisdom by paying it forward to others who may have to face the same challenges you have. You can help them by reminding them about the joy in all of this.

For anyone facing hard choices, I offer this:
It doesn't matter how old you are, how much the odds are against you, or how tough the social pressure and mental angst may seem. If you create your own path based on joy and gratitude, then do what it takes to keep moving forward, you will realize your vision. And in this way, you will change the world.

CHAPTER · 5

How to Cultivate Intuition

Maybe you are in a position like I was, where somewhere along the line you 'forgot' about your intuition. For me, when it finally came knocking on my door, I didn't know if I could or should trust it.

If I can't trust myself fully, that makes decision making more difficult and more time-consuming. What I wanted to know was: can I learn to trust my intuition? Can using intuition make decision making faster? The answer is yes, and yes.

If you have these three conditions around your decision, you can absolutely trust your intuition.[44]

1. A controlled, regular environment.
2. Immediate feedback on the outcome of your decision.
3. A lot of practice.

There are some real-life situations where people can 'learn' intuition under these conditions. That is to say, a person can practice decision making under these three conditions and feel confident in acting on their intuition alone.

Developing intuition in playing chess is one case. Highly structured conditions, immediate feedback with each play decision, lots of decisions involved in every game. Chess masters must learn to play by intuition, because there is a time limit for making moves; they just can't spend all day making calculations and assessing patterns. They learn to put repeated, trusted, successful strategies and maneuvers into their subconscious.

Some people feel that deeply bonded couples can trust their intuition on each other's moods. Again, repeated, trusted successful strategies are right there in an instant.

How about developing intuition for something as scientific as diagnosing melanoma?[45] Yep! There is an application that can train dermatologists how to intuitively diagnose melanoma.

Our application, called Skinder, teaches intuitive visual diagnosis of melanoma by quickly presenting learners with thousands of benign and malignant skin lesions. Users make rapid binary decisions by swiping right for benign or left for malignant, and then receive instant feedback on accuracy. With this application, learners can amass a mental repository of diagnostic experience in a short amount of time.

Dr. Kolodney, developer of application that
trains intuitive diagnosis

So are the intuitive diagnoses as good as the studied analytically informed diagnoses? The answer is yes; in fact, the results of intuitive diagnosis are even better! In one study the resulting diagnosis done by intuition was correct almost 10% more of the time than the analysis-informed diagnosis.

To be fair, most of the decisions we make are definitely not in a 'regular environment'. We are out in the mess of life that is filled with complexity, ambiguity and uncertainty. As a result, our intuition can yield both successful and unsuccessful outcomes.

Just like strategies we employ to fend off the human reality of cognitive bias, there are strategies for how to improve how we use our intuition.

Strategy #1: Intuition Benchmarking

A great starting place is simply to observe your own decision process and look for the events in that decision where your intuition shined through. When is your intuition shining? Look for the joy, acceptance, trust, gratitude and sense of ownership in the decision. I provided an example of this in the first chapter, when we walked through the decision to get a new job. We make so many decisions in any given day, you can do this reflection at any time. It doesn't have to be a top-level tough decision, just one where you made a solid conscious choice. For example: did you choose to bring a reusable bag into the grocery store? Why did you do that? Were you solving a specific problem? Was that decision a reflection of a value or belief you have? Did it benefit just yourself or others? Are you grateful you made that decision? Did someone prompt you do it, or did you choose to do it on your own accord? Were you confident you do the necessary steps to see this decision through? Were the results of that decision good? Did you feel proud or happy with the results? Is there anything you do to own that decision going forward? Is this decision something you have always done or is it a new practice?

Track when you apply your intuition to make decisions.

Take a moment and make a little note that describes how happy and grateful you are about making a decision with the full power of choice working for you! It might sound something like this: *I am so happy and grateful I listen to my values around doing my part to reduce plastic in the world. I keep reusable bags in my car, so I can consistently use them when I grocery shop.*

You can jot this down in your notebook, or if it's more your style, post a picture or meme, or put a sticky note on the fridge. It doesn't matter how you do it, what's important is that it's written down so you can reference a growing collection of you making great decisions. This will help you:

- Identify improvements that might be made on subsequent uses of your intuition.
- Grow confidence in trusting your intuition.

There are many ways to journal your intuitive moments and the results you have from acting on them. Take pictures and make a meme. Write a sticky note and put it on the fridge. If you like highly structured tracking, you can augment the options tracker you already started.

For more complex decisions, you may prefer to use more highly structured tracking. In the options tracker used in the previous chapter, we have an example of moving locations with a new job. Where we left off with adding trustworthiness, it looked like this:

Option	Honest	Competent	Reliable	Preferences & Joy Align	Keep or Reject
Acme in NE	Yes	Yes	Yes	Yes	Go forward
Jo's Co in LA	Yes	Yes	No	No—$ No— spouse	Reject: Spouse not onboard

Now just augment it to include what you learned and the results:

Option	Trustworthy?	Self-Knowlege & Joy Aligns?	Keep or Reject?	Results & Learning
Acme in NE	Honest–Y Competent–Y Reliable–Yes	Yes	Go forward	Met all goals! Priority list made negotiations easy
Jo's Co in LA	Honest–Y Reliable–N No–$	No–spouse $ No–spouse	*Reject: spouse not onboard*	Spot-on intuition about spouse happiness

Strategy #2: Practice Recognizing and Using Your Intuition

Practice, Practice, Practice

There are a couple of ways of going about receiving information from your intuition:

1. You can purposefully call on your intuition, or
2. Your intuition can call on you.

Either way, make the time and give yourself the freedom to nurture your intuition. You'll want to try it out and practice often because trusting your intuition enables you to take advantage of your inner wisdom. It's there, just waiting for you to choose it!

> Intuition has the use-it-or-lose-it quality, just like our muscles and thinking do, so purposefully choosing to develop your intuition is necessary.

Don't forget to do the thinking part first and *then* open up to the feeling. Remember the little mantra for making decisions with both analysis and intuition? Even when you practice, keep the use of intuition in that order.

Think-Feel-Choose-Act
One for the money, two for the show, three to get ready and four to go!

I've trusted the still, small voice of intuition my entire life and the only time I've made mistakes is when I didn't listen.

Oprah Winfrey

When Your Intuition Calls on You

Your intuition may be signaling you that even though a decision seems logical, it won't bring you closer to your core goals. This makes sense, since intuition is your clear, calm inner wisdom that knows what is truly right—it is doing its job to remind you of your values (your Joy story).

If your intuition is reaching out to you it will probably come in some very tangible, visceral body sensations like: sweating, a knot in your stomach, a change in your heartrate or breathing, muscle tension, tingling, etc. It's worth pointing out body sensations are not always a warning of something bad, just a communication. I often times have a body response when my intuition is really positively excited about something in a good way: I may cry, tremble, bounce my legs or feet, suddenly feel like running, jumping or hugging.

The practice is simple—choose to listen to this.

Take note of what is going on. And then make time to take a quiet break and reflect.

When You Call upon Your Intuition

We have already covered a few ways to call upon your intuition when we talked about Bias Busters. Remember establishing a Space to Breathe? This is about setting aside a time and a place to let your thoughts settle so there is room for your intuition to enter. It's a good idea that this place be a calm and quiet one so you can focus on receiving the intuitive information—sometimes we call this 'listening' to our intuition. My favorite places for this are my car, my shower, my yoga room (on my meditation cushion), or walking in the forest.

Create a time and a space for receiving your intuition.

111

Intentionally Calm and Clear Your Thoughts

Once you are there in your Space to Breathe, intentionally quiet yourself and your mind. One technique, that now has scientific studies that prove what yoga practitioners have known for thousands of years, is paying attention to your breathing. Doing a few simple breathing exercises will effectively calm you.

A recent scientific term that describes this is: *Cardiac coherence breathing exercises*. Yoga breath control practice is called *Pranayama*, and it is used in this case to stimulate the parasympathetic nervous system (the feeling part of you) and divert attention from the thinking part of you.[46] Once you are in that 'state', all that is left is to take notice of what arises.

When you allow time to slow down in order for your intuition to find you, you arrive at a decision more quickly. By relaxing your mind and accessing your deeper consciousness, the answer is already there waiting for you.[47]

Rick Synder, intuitive leadership consultant
and author

Another technique for calming and settling thought that has been used for decades by psychologists is spending some creative time with an adult coloring book. According to the American Art Therapy Association, the process of making and creating artwork can be used to "foster self-awareness and improve reality orientation".[48] There is the additional benefit of explicitly practicing intuitive decisions as you select your approach to coloring.

Want to get started right away? I have included a Pocket Adult Coloring Book at the end of this publication. Each image has a suggested meditation. Just pull out your colored pencils and give it a try. Go ahead, and practice making space for your intuition right now.

Make the Decision to Practice Every Day

What we are talking about here is growing the ability to win the head-game. This is mind training and the key is consistency. Establishing a regular routine is helpful and I recommend like many people, to make it a morning thing.

A Sample Morning Practice

Waking up

Interestingly enough, to do a daily practice, you actually have to get out of bed. For me, a lifelong snooze button addict, this was a serious challenge. For the first week of my practice I committed only to this: when the alarm went off, I would flop myself out of bed, sit quietly and drink a cup of herbal tea.

Yep. That's it. This was surprisingly difficult for me and an important ground zero procedure. I have been waking up my entire life—getting the kids ready for daycare and school, getting me ready for work. Honestly, I thought I was a pro at it.

This was different. This was waking up to be peaceful and joyful: Not waking to rush into the day, but waking to train my mind.

113

As I struggled with this change, I noticed that what made it difficult for me was the dark and the cold that met me outside of the covers. I didn't want that to get in my way so I got a few luxury items to help along the transition to starting my day with warmth.

Helpful Items For Waking Up

- Sunrise alarm clock (with wake-up light and nature sounds)
- Lemon water
- Organic herbal tea (chai, ginger and turmeric)
- Electric boiler (with timer)
- Sitting shawl (natural fiber)
- Warm socks
- Space heater (with timer and oscillation)
- Meditation cushion (firm and elevating)
- Mantra ("Om Gam Ganapataye Namaha")

Preparation

The best preparation for a morning practice really begins the night before. In the words of my yoga teacher, "Bookend your day in warmth." Consider approaching this very literally. Get your eyes off screens at least an hour before bedtime. Take a warm shower or bath to calm your thoughts. Rub oil on your body and your feet and enjoy a peaceful night's sleep.

That said, in preparation for morning practice, I chose to try and train myself to poop every day upon waking. Now the first time this was suggested to me, I giggled to myself at how unrealistic that is: pooping on command was only something I had trained my Doberman to do! That said, daily pooping was on my naturopath's set of things to strive for in gut health, so I decided to give it an honest try. The Ayurvedic position of pooping is squatting, with your thighs pressing into your belly, and then you relax, exhale and suck your belly button in and up. This also seemed very impossible to me. There was no position I could get into where my thighs touched my abdomen and balancing on my toilet was just not going to happen: yes, I did try, failed and laughed very loudly! At that point, I didn't even get to try the notion of sucking in my belly button. What I was successful in was getting a squatting toilet stool and consistently using it.

Another, much easier preparation for morning practice is the commitment to tongue scraping. The idea of removing that morning mucus coating off my tongue just sounded right, and I had been brushing my tongue my whole life; this just sounded more thorough. And if it did 'promote overall digestive health,' that was just a great bonus in my mind.

Combine Moving and Breathing: Pawanmuktasana Series 1

This practice is designed for anyone; young or old, healthy or sick, physically strong or weak. It doesn't matter. It is all done in a seated position. So even when (especially when) I'm not feeling well, I still do this practice. I could feel the benefit of it immediately and accumulatively. It was easy to notice that this made a positive difference in how my day started. Overall, this practice brought about a profound change in my life: if you choose to do only one yoga practice, I recommend this one.

You can read the full description of the Pawanmuktasana Series in the incredibly comprehensive illustrated yoga manual, "Asana Pranayama Mudra Bandha." Pawanmuktasana is described as "a group of asanas that remove any blockages which prevent the free flow of energy in the body and mind." My yoga teacher taught me to do a practice that is similarly described in the Pawanmuktasana Series Part 1 of this book, with the movements done with synchronized breathing and prana awareness breaks. She added a breathing exercise at the end that involves inhaling fully and holding the breath in and sipping it in even further until finally it's necessary to fully exhale.

If you are interested in trying out this yoga practice, please connect with a qualified hatha yoga instructor. That said, you can get an idea about what this is by searching videos on the internet. I have yet to find a free video that demonstrates the integrated breathing as I was taught; you might want to look into online subscription offerings.

So as soon as I learned Pawanmuktasana, I incorporated it into my daily waking up practice. I spent less time waking up and drinking tea so I had time to move and breathe through this series. As my own choice, typically I did a full version of this on the weekends (20-30 minutes) and a shortened version of it (5-10 minutes) during the working week days.

Mantra: instrument of thought

Mantra was a complete surprise to me, in that it apparently is the essence of mind training. Developed before language, sources do not agree on what mantra is. I follow the thinking of my yoga instructor, that it is a prayer and divine vibration. There are many mantra ranging from a single syllable to long phrases.

I chose to pick just one to focus on, the Ganesh mantra, "Om Gam Ganapataye Namaha." I chose this mantra because I love the image of an elephant-headed deity removing obstacles for me!

As soon as I learned the Ganesh mantra, I incorporated it into my daily waking up practice. I found a song version of this on YouTube that I enjoy, and play it while I do my bathroom asana preparation time. It repeats 108 times and takes about six minutes to go through.

It is not advised that you multi-task with mantra. However, I find it comforting to chant as a 'background' activity and especially enjoy chanting it while I am in the shower.

Gratitude

At the end of each morning practice, I take moment to thank—just whatever thanking that seems to arise.

Summary of my daily morning practice

When all the steps of my new daily yoga practice came together, it looked like this:

1. Get a good night's sleep.
2. Get out of bed.
3. Space heater on to warm my yoga mat.
4. Drink a cup of warm lemon water (electric pot already had my water hot).
5. Listen and sing along with the Ganesh mantra. (6 minutes)
6. Poop using squatty potty and bidet.
7. Brush my teeth and scrape my tongue.
8. Sit on my meditation cushion with my cozy shawl and finish my tea and mantra.
9. Do Pawanmuktasana with breath exercise. (5-20 minutes)
10. Savor a moment of gratitude.

After just a couple weeks of consistently doing this, it wasn't hard to notice the immediate and continuous expansion of peace of mind, my sense of self-acceptance and my feeling of general wellness.

CHAPTER · 6

WHAT A DECISION COACH
DOES AND DOESN'T DO

We are often called upon to help others make decisions. Maybe you're helping elderly parents with the decision to sell their house and move into assisted living. Or your lifelong friend is counting on you for support in the decision to get a divorce. Perhaps you've been called upon by a family member who is choosing whether (or not) to address medical conditions or select treatment options. This comes at us from all directions at any time. Maybe you have been tasked with enabling your employees to improve their critical thinking skills and to exercise independent decision making in an expanded set of work-related situations.

In these scenarios, you are looking at decision making from a different perspective. **Now, you are the decision coach.**

The key thing to remember when a trusted friend or family member asks for your decision-making help: *you are not making the decision for them!*

They may even explicitly ask you to make their decision (Prairie Chicken Pippen comes to mind), or maybe you can barely help yourself from *wanting* to make it for them, but the approach you want to take is to be their advocate, and *not* their delegate.

> Be their advocate, not their delegate.

Think of all that practice it takes to build the critical thinking and intuitive thinking muscles; do not deprive that person of the opportunity to grow stronger! They can do it!

As your loved one's decision coach, your role is to be their advocate, encouraging and helping them to fulfill their specific desires. You want to help your friend have a safe, memorable and empowering experience. You are in the privileged position to make a positive impact during the hard work of bringing about change.

Okay, this is sounding kind of hard—why did they reach out to me again?

> Your friend is counting on you to help them balance their brain's response to uncertainty.

Here is a list of some things you can do for your trusting friend before, during, and after the transformation they desire.

Seven Ways to Advocate for Their Tough Decisions

1. Don't make their decisions.
   - Foster action-based thinking and independent decision making.
2. Help them know what they want.
   - Communicate their preferences to themselves, and to those who will help in the process of bringing about change.
   - Help balance their fear response with a process of deciding.

    • Help them feel comfortable with the situation they are currently in, and/or will be in as they move through the plan of action.

3. Help them to know what they know and don't know.
   - Help them acknowledge entrenched views and acknowledge bias that might not be serving them well.
   - Help them research options and evaluate them for fit with their preferences.
   - Help them to understand if the people they are considering as solution providers are trustworthy.
   - Help them to understand procedures, possible complications or risks.

4. Help them trust their intuition and when to apply it.
   - Teach them the mantra: Think-Feel-Choose-Act.
   - Encourage them to make space to calm and clear their thoughts and respond to the power of their inner wisdom.
   - Help them to weave their gut feelings into decisions and create a track record of results.

5. Help them focus on what's important.
   - Help them develop a plan of action.
   - Be sure their plan includes measurements, tangible thank you moments, and lots of space for joy-filled activities: being a trusted friend, this might be an area of extra expertise and focus for you!

6. Help them to understand what is involved in owning the change they desire.

7. If mutually agreed, during the transition time, you can complement or completely free your friend's significant other from tasks in the event you are better suited, or in a better position to do so.

When You Must Decide for a Significant Other

A recent study by the Yale School of Medicine shows that spouses who were making medical decisions for their significant other got it right only 21 percent of the time.[49] The learning from this? If you want to represent your significant other well, you must take time to share joys and desires with each other. Know each other's preferences in general, and especially those associated with big decision moments.

Special Note to Professional Decision Facilitators: Business Analysts

Did you even realize how important your role is in getting things done? You are the team's decision coach for every project you are assigned to. The BABOK v3 says "Business Analysis is the practice of enabling change in an enterprise."

I know I am not alone in the idea that facilitating decision making is your role as a business analyst.

Many people view decision making as a tool in your toolbox; I view it as your role. One of the main responsibilities of business analysis is to help others make better decisions. If decisions are not made during a project, nothing gets done.

Jonathan Kupersmith, co-author of *Business Analysis for Dummies*[50]

I encourage you to augment your standard training by folding intuition, including intuition tracking, into your existing best practices. Wouldn't it be nice if we could get this formally acknowledged by the IIBA and inserted into the next version of the BABOK? How about with the Project Management Institute too?! If you have passion or interest in seeing these kinds of changes, please contact me! Meanwhile, I hope you enjoy a new and exciting approach to your work as you weave intuition into your everyday role and activities of facilitating decision making.

CHAPTER · 7

HOW TO CREATE MOMENTS
FOR KIDS TO EXPLORE CHOICE

How to make decisions is a life skill, one that can be taught.[51]

A young adult who has practiced critical thinking, problem solving, and innovation has a tremendous competitive advantage in today's increasingly complex and competitive world.

As parents, we owe it to our kids to augment what is taught in the school system and intentionally create everyday moments that foster fair-minded independent thinking (both critical and intuitive), problem solving, and how to listen to their inner voice.

Intuition and independent decision making can be 'trained out' of children if they are told adults are always right. People can become intuition-challenged if they do not grow emotionally, continuously live in fear of danger or abuse, and never learn to trust themselves or others.

There are many things we can do to grow thinking and feeling skills in our kids and others around us.

In all those years at school, not once did I take a class that taught me how to make a complex decision, despite the fact that the ability to make informed and creative decisions is a skill that applies to every aspect of our lives.

Steven Johnson[52]

Discuss Attitudes Toward Thinking

Observe out loud real-life examples when people display naïve, selfish and fair-minded attitudes in their decisions and actions. This will open an opportunity to talk about values and beliefs. Allow your child to express their feelings about what kind of attitude they want to have and how that affects others around them. Discuss how that affects themselves and talk openly about regret.

Help Discover Approaches to Problem Resolution

When your child comes to you with a problem, empathize but don't solve the issue. Be involved in helping them find an approach to resolution and then support them in the execution of that approach.

Share Gratitude for Recent Choices

Take time together every day to feel thankful for decisions. Talk about or write down a few things they appreciate about their choice. Consider posting this on the refrigerator as another accomplishment to be proud of. Model and teach a giving thanks ritual. This can come in many forms: meditation, prayer times, in sending thank you notes for presents, etc. Let them define a way they would like to share gratitude. Encourage them to feel thankful even before they have received something they desire.

Practice Thought-Calming and Inner Voice Listening

Help the child listen to herself, encourage reflection. Practice with them various techniques on how to calm their thoughts and listen to their own inner voice. Raise awareness of opportunities for them to learn how to make more efficient and satisfying decisions.

Create Decision Experience Opportunities

The best way to support your child in developing decision skills is to create experience opportunities for them. It is well understood how learning chess and playing other highly structured games that introduce repetitive decision making with immediate feedback can help a child build heuristic intuition and confidence in their play. But what about experiencing messy real-life decision practice? With a little creativity and a sense of adventure, you can create structured events, so kids can have a safe space to be curious, explore, select from a narrowed set of options, succeed or fail, learn, and keep on going. Many of my best memories are based on just these kinds of constructs.

Option Complexity Practice while Grocery Shopping

Since grocery shopping is a regular activity, it is easy to set up kids for plenty of decision making practice. Before hitting the aisles, talk about preferences like nutritional value, cost, sourcing, condition of produce, time to prepare, packaging, family member preferences, etc. When you get to a section with a lot of options you can narrow the choice appropriately for the age of the child. In the beginning, the

127

instruction might be: pick the ketchup that is least expensive with no sugar. As they get more practiced, the instruction might be wider: pick the ketchup that matches our agreed upon preferences. They can practice advocating for someone else in the family by providing the instruction, which ketchup do you think your sister would like? (We ended up with purple ketchup frequently).

When there is no clear match, you can talk about how they feel about one choice or the other. They can start to notice how they are influenced by marketing. They can understand how their decision making must be efficient when there are many items to select. As a bonus, this is a great time to practice math and budgeting! You can even put them in charge of a calculator. A strategy my friend shared with me is to give your child the list of items they are in charge of with a total dollar limit. Each item's cost is punched into the calculator and when the dollar limit is reached, it's time to check out. You can imagine some trial and error in selections will affect if and how they can select everything on their list, or maybe even have room for a bonus item at the end.

Making a series of small decisions will help her learn to make pros and cons quickly and get into the habit of decision-making.

Kate Rope, award winning journalist[53]

CRITICAL THINKING PRACTICE WITH THE SCIENTIFIC METHOD

Science is a great way for kids to learn about how a process can help them make meaningful discoveries driven by their own curiosity. Encourage your kid to gain experiences with this way of thinking by participating in a science fair.

We need as many scientifically literate people as we can in our society so that when it comes time to vote and make decisions about our future, we do it in an informed way.[54]

Bill Nye, The Science Guy

In my first science fair, I got the idea from reading that smoking was bad for you, then proved it to myself. Chances are, this experience in practicing critical thinking saved my dad's life.

My dad was a chain smoker and it was well understood in the family that cigarettes created sticky messes to clean up. It started at the grocery store, where we went to the aisle I wasn't allowed in and purchased very specific brand of cigarettes (it wasn't the least expensive one, which always baffled me). That carton was one of the most expensive things in the cart! I could have had several boxes of Captain Crunch if it were not for that carton. I was regularly tasked with scrubbing the smoke and tar off the inside of the windshield of my dad's work truck. We also had to repaint the ceiling above my dad's recliner in the living room. It took only one trip to the library to see pictures of tarry sticky slime on someone's lungs. Those dismembered lungs were so disgusting and black, frankly, I had a hard time believing that was a real photograph of a real actual person.

When science fair time came around I asked my dad if he would help me with an experiment to prove whether that picture was telling the truth. The idea was for him to smoke through filters for one month. The first filter for one day's smoking. The second filter for two days' smoking, etc. So a total of seven filters over twenty-eight days. If the filters got progressively dark with tar, I would know the same was happening to his lungs and the picture was true. Amazingly, he agreed to this.

I knew what I wanted to find out, I created a plan, we did the hard work of following the plan (my dad actually suffered incredibly, as he tells the tale) and we considered the results—yes, that last filter was black. We made the conclusion that indeed, those blackened lungs were representing the reality of a smoker's body, and as a result, my dad quit smoking cold turkey. Today he is eighty-six. Based on a goal, some curiosity, and a plan, we made a change in our world. This fueled my passion for using science for bringing about transformation.

Course Correction Practice Taking an Uncharted Road trip

I wanted to go on a road trip with my son as a fun way we could spend time together while my daughter was at scout camp. So together, we agreed to design a travel experiment.

I would set up the overall boundaries, including the goal of him learning to read a map, and he got to choose the destination, how we got there and back and any activities in between.

The cost guideline was there could be only one hotel night stay and any activity prices had to be in the range of free to no more than the cost of going to the local science museum (my personal favorite destination, yes, I was trying to bias his choice).

With this construct in place, he figured out we could go to Alcatraz.

His innovation kind of surprised me, because it required we stay a night at his aunt and uncle's place in addition to one hotel night.

Creative, social, and still within the construct I put together. Clearly this was going to be *his* road trip!

After stopping by the local AAA, I handed him the map and one goal of arriving at our hotel in San Francisco some time before we couldn't stay awake any longer. Anything in between was up to him. So we were off. There was really only one highway to take to start with, so he focused his efforts on planning a picnic lunch in the mountains at a rest stop/camping ground. While there, he cut his thumb with a pocket knife; it was kind of nasty. First course correction: a side trip to get stitches at the next city. That turned out to be its own adventure, but we didn't let it throw us off track. With stitches and too much sterile wrapping, we went forward to Alcatraz!

Soon we got to where there were some road options. He directed me to take an exit that went in the completely wrong way. We were unfamiliar with the area so it was hard to know if we were indeed off track. We looked for milestone cities and intersections, and sure enough, he concluded that this road would never get us to San Francisco by the end of the day: the last navigation step was a mistake. A fail.

He looked a little worried for a moment, but I assured him that's how we figure things out! We had all the tools we needed to get back on track. I narrowed the options a bit for him. We could either turn around and go back to where we got off track, or find another path in the right direction. After spending a little quality time with the map, he found a way around that was *not* backtracking and to our happy surprise landed us at an In-and-Out Burger just when we were hungry again. Back on track and well fed!

After this glorious recovery the game was on! From there on he understood we were all okay with making some mistakes along the way but still needed to be accountable for moving forward toward our important goals. He also understood there could be unexpected *pleasant* surprises along the way, even if under uncertain conditions.

Yes, we got the hotel safely that night, and we did find our way to Alcatraz. I think I still have a souvenir somewhere. Now with the success of reaching and enjoying our primary destination, we had plenty of time for freewheeling exploration.

On the way home, he chose to head into the countryside where we ran into a farm with the sweetest strawberries I have had in my life (seriously), which also had a huge corn maze. He decided we would accept the challenge of trying to complete it in under forty-five minutes, which was the current mazing record. I admit I was a little worried—that was the hardest damn corn maze I had ever heard of.

> By this time, my son's ability to course correct was on fire!

He came up with the idea of us jogging the whole way (oh, great), and when there were two direction options we split up in each direction, but with consistent voice pings of "Marco Polo." The first person to find a dead end would run back to the other person's location. He was *good* at this! Yes, we created a new record at forty-three minutes, which even impressed the slightly scary farmer that reminded us of a Scooby Doo character. Were we (mostly me) grateful for my son's decisions in that maze? You bet!

The route home needed to be fast, so we stuck to the major highway. However he had a great eye for finding the exits to the Krispy Cremes and In-and-Out's along the way. On our road trip, navigated entirely by a ten-year-old: sure, we got to Alcatraz and he learned to use a map, but that was trivial compared to the fun we had practicing thinking together.

Innovation Practice at the Library

When I was a kid, my mom took me and my brother to the public library on Saturdays. This was a big event, involving a thirty-minute drive into the city downtown area and a special treat afterwards. The thing I loved about it was I had free rein of what I did there as long as I stayed within the pre-established preferences and boundaries.

I could check out as many books as I could carry (some trial and error was required to figure out my personal max was about eleven books). I had to follow the library rules, which was fine with me since the sounds of whispers and muffled voices intrigued me. I could get a book from any section, and I could go anywhere in the building within the amount of time set by my mom. The choice-making opportunities were everywhere! Kids' section or adult? Mess around with my brother or adventure on my own? Fiction section or non-fiction? Science shelves or the philosophy shelves? Books with pictures or without? Spend my time browsing books or look up something specific in the card catalogue? Hang out in the study carrels or flop right down in the middle of the aisles? Be curious about new stuff or stick to the topics I knew from before and enjoy them more?

This was great choice-making practice, complete with dealing with complexity in options, practicing quiet calmness, and there was immediate feedback on my choice of actions. I noticed a trend in my choices: that I spent most of my time exploring the shelves in the 500 section and became fascinated with how math described nature, which seemed like a secret code representing the voice of God. Occasionally I would slip over to the 600 section of how computers helped us with math, though I had never seen a computer in real life. My all-time favorite book was called "The Pediatrician". My name was on that checkout card many times. It showed in large color photographs how humans transform from what looks like a little bean into a fully formed baby, all while in the dark, deep inside the warm nurturing environment of the mother.

And so my obsession with transformation began.

Terrie Novak is a business systems analyst and made a career in facilitating software development teams through the thousands of decisions needed to deliver products to market. She developed a unique framework that integrates both analysis and intuition, allowing decisions to come from a position of personal choice.

We can hack the same techniques used to manage uncertainty in digital product development to help us through our own choice making challenges.

Decision Doctor is Terrie's second book and has a companion online course designed for anyone who would like to overcome doubt and improve the quality of their decisions. This online forum provides the opportunity to work through your own real-life tough decisions, while developing a daily practice that cultivates your innate choice-making power.

Also, by Terrie Novak: *Hypothesis: An HPV Healing Experiment.* This book encourages and supports women as they face the tough decisions associated with the diagnosis of HPV and cervical dysplasia.

Terrie holds a bachelors degree in Physics from East Carolina University. She has attained professional certifications in Business Analysis (CBAP), Project Management (PMP), Architecture (TOGAF), and Agile Methodology (Certified PO).

You can explore her website (www.terrienovak.com) or follow Terrie on Instagram (@theterrienovak) and other social media.

ACKNOWLEDGEMENTS

Friend me: (Do I really have friends who have been my besties for over 40 years?) Kathy, Peggy, Sue[55]—you have been my decision coaches many times over the years and during some of the most pivotal moments of my life. Thank you for being there for me, every time, including when I had the crazy idea of being an author.

Daughter me: (Lucky, lucky me, I sure didn't earn this one!) Mom and Dad, I am one of those rare people who had the most loving and supportive childhood imaginable. The only problem is I don't have any repressed issues to blame for anything! To this day you continue to inspire me and model courageous love. Your support and encouragement are unwavering, even when I write books that have sex parts that make you laugh in all the wrong places. Thank you for teaching me about the strength of love and joy.

Family me: (So, I kind of roped them in, but . . .) Lynn, Todd, Aunt Ginger, Carol, Danielle, Bear—thank you for always being willing to put energy into listening to me obsess over ideas and for your valuable feedback that is always a warm weave of encouragement and possibility.

Mentored me: (There's got to be some pay-it-forward coming on soon.) Thank you, Karl Wiegers of Process Impact, for challenging me to "write the book that needs to be written," and for encouraging me to explore that all elusive design moment. It's not a single thing or point in time is it? Just a series of decisions that seems to have little respect for stage-gates or sign-offs. So much gratitude to you, Britt Steele, for teaching me how to form a daily practice to nourish my buddhi and for enabling me to see what I needed most was to trust my inner voice.

Self-publishing me: (so many people!) It's funny they call it self-publishing when so many people joyfully engaged in making this book happen. Lynn Marie, collaborating with you is literally a dream come true, thank you for adding so much beauty to these pages with your thoughtful and engaging illustrations that just beg to be colored. Thank you, Shannon Page, for your editing skills and kindness. Jaye Manus of QA Productions, thank you for your creativity in interior book design (sure we can do tables and fill-in-the-blanks in e-books), and having the patience to deal with all those end notes I love so much. Thank you, Maggie Ziomek, for the book cover that inspires professionalism and somehow magically conveys the balance of thinking and feeling. Emily Mercer Beauty and Jennifer Alyse Photography, you not only made me look great but feel great when I was so dang far out of my comfort zone in front of a camera.

Receiving me: Thank you to the dedicated professionals referenced in this book who have studied why and how we think, feel, choose and act. Your ability to see the truth inspires me. I am honored to take a small part in the learning and teaching of your findings.

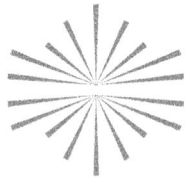

Coloring Meditation

If you don't already have a meditation practice, or if you are looking for new ideas, coloring is a fun option to explore.

For me, coloring reminds me of my carefree childhood, which brings me into a great state of being. I like to use colored pencils; I enjoy the options of shading, sharpness and layering they give me. I feel grateful for the time I have to just . . . color.

This is a playful way to practice many "micro decisions" and see the immediate feedback of those choices right in front of you. What image do you choose? Will you choose to follow the meditation suggestions or do it differently? What will you color with? Where will you do this activity? Will you finish a whole image in one sitting? Will you try and multitask while coloring? What will you do if you don't like the coloring you just did? Did you daydream while coloring or were you focused?

You get the idea. Try it out. I would love it if you shared some of your coloring! How about on Instagram? Tag @theterrienovak or #decisiondoctor. Describe how it made you feel or think.

Meditation: Woman with Universe

Sound: breath

Motion: gentle circle or spin

Scent: air after rain and lightening

Gratitude: for time to receive

MEDITATION: GREEN MAN

Sound: footsteps

Motion: walking, arms swinging

Scent: flowering magnolia tree

Gratitude: for time to appreciate

MEDITATION: ORDER IN CHAOS

Sound: rustling of twigs

Motion: twist and untwist

Scent: tree bark and sap

Gratitude: for time to plan

MEDITATION: GROWTH IN DECAY

Sound: water flowing

Motion: stretching upward and
downward

Scent: earthy fungus

Gratitude: for time to learn

MEDITATION: BRIGHT AND BOLD

Sound: hum

Motion: rocking side to side

Scent: sweetness

Gratitude: for time to start fresh

REFERENCES

What School Never Taught You About Critical Thinking

[1] Zameena Mejia: "Amazon's Jeff Bezos: This simple framework can help you answer the most difficult questions you face"
www.cnbc.com/2018/11/19/jeff-bezos-simple-strategy-for-answering-amazons-hardest-questions--.html

[2] Business Analysis Body of Knowledge
www.iiba.org/standards-and-resources/babok/

[3] Daniel Kahneman

[4] Easy Bake Oven
www.youtube.com/watch?v=XcY0ghee5Sc

[5] Holly Green: "How to Develop 5 Critical Thinking Types"
www.forbes.com/sites/work-in-progress/2012/03/27/how-to-develop-5-critical-thinking-types/#4b219aa8ef0a

[6] For readers who are not heavily influenced by the 1970's Reeses ad campaign, you may need to watch this to understand the header "Two great tastes that taste great together"
www.youtube.com/watch?v=GuENAWds5B0

[7] Meta-analytic Investigations of the Relation Between Intuition and Analysis, Yi Wang Scott Highhouse Christopher J. Lake Nicole L. Petersen Thaddeus B. Rada
onlinelibrary.wiley.com/doi/full/10.1002/bdm.1903

[8] How to Make Better Decisions

www.discoverbusiness.us/resources/problem-solving/

[9] Three attitudes based on descriptions found on criticalthinking.org

[10] Dr. Mehran Sahami: "Nine Tips for Smarter Decision-Making"

stanfordmag.org/contents/nine-tips-for-smarter-decision-making?utm_source=mag_twitter&utm_medium=social_click&utm_content=nine-tips-for-smarter-decision-making

[11a] Chewbacca mask hawked at insane prices on Amazon and Ebay.

www.nydailynews.com/entertainment/movies/chewbacca-mask-sells-online-viral-facebook-video-article-1.2646757

GOOD DECISIONS BAD OUTCOMES

[11] Natasha Tracy: "What are the Cognitive Symptoms (Deficits) in Depression?"

www.healthyplace.com/depression/symptoms/what-are-the-cognitive-symptoms-deficits-in-depression

[12] Dr. Eva Krockow: "How Many Decisions Do We Make Each Day?"

www.psychologytoday.com/us/blog/stretching-theory/201809/how-many-decisions-do-we-make-each-day

[13] Svetlana Whitener: "The Difference Between Making A Choice And A Decision", Forbes

www.forbes.com/sites/forbescoachescouncil/2017/05/19/the-difference-between-making-a-choice-and-a-decision/#1ab03dca4b7a

[14] Dan Ariely: "Are we in control of our own decisions?", Ted Talks

www.ted.com/talks/dan_ariely_asks_are_we_in_control_of_our_own_decisions?language=en

[15] List of Optical Illusions, Wikipedia.org

en.wikipedia.org/wiki/List_of_optical_illusions

[16] Jeff Desjardine: "Every Single Cognitive Bias in One Infographic"

www.visualcapitalist.com/every-single-cognitive-bias/

[17]   Peer J Inc: "Measuring online social bubbles"
peerj.com/articles/cs-38/

[18]   theconversation.com/us

[19]   Giovanni Luca Ciampaglia: "Biases Make People Vulnerable to Misinformation Spread by Social Media", Scientific American
www.scientificamerican.com/article/biases-make-people-vulnerable-to-misinformation-spread-by-social-media/

[20]   from Indiana University: Stephanie Pappas: "When You Go with Your Gut, You Feel Like You"
www.livescience.com/63535-gut-decisions-true-self.html?utm_source=twitter&utm_medium=social

[21]   Dan Gilbert: "Why we make bad decisions", Ted Talks
www.ted.com/talks/dan_gilbert_researches_happiness?language=en

You Vs. Brain Bias: How to Win the Battle of Cognitive Illusions

[22]   Nora Batelle: "The One Easy Trick That Will Sharpen Your Decision-Making"
thriveglobal.com/stories/the-one-easy-trick-that-will-sharpen-your-decision-making/

[23]   "Why Curiosity Matters", Harvard Business Review
hbr.org/2018/09/curiosity

[24]   Curiosity.merkgroup.com
www.youtube.com/watch?v=L7vnWISreAI

[25]   "States of Curiosity Modulate Hippocampus-Dependent Learning via the Dopaminergic Circuit", Neuron
www.cell.com/neuron/abstract/S0896-6273(14)00804-6

[26]   Dan M. Kahan: "Science Curiosity and Political Information Processing"
papers.ssrn.com/sol3/papers.cfm?abstract_id=2816803

[27]   Tom Belger: "Poker champ wows Davos with the secret of smart decision-making"
finance.yahoo.com/news/poker-champ-wows-davos-secret-smart-decision-making-163950133.html

[28]   Observer effect, Wikipedia
en.wikipedia.org/wiki/Observer_effect_(physics)

[29]   Evan Polman, Business Insider: "The best way to make a decision is either by having someone choose for you or by pretending you're choosing for someone else, says one business school professor."
www.businessinsider.com/make-good-decision-pretend-to-choose-for-someone-else-2018-12

[30]   Gary Klein: "Performing a Project Premortem"
hbr.org/2007/09/performing-a-project-premortem

[31]   Before You Make that Big Decision, Kahneman, Lovallo, Sibony, June 2011 Harvard Business Review
hbr.org/2011/06/the-big-idea-before-you-make-that-big-decision

[32]   D. Kahneman: "A Nobel Prize-winning psychologist says the most successful decision-makers know how to use their gut feelings in a way the rest of us don't"
www.businessinsider.com/make-good-decision-delay-intuition-daniel-kahneman-2018-12

THREE DECISION MAKING STRATEGIES THAT REALLY WORK

[33]   George T. James: "Courage in Decision-Making", James Consulting Group
thinkinthingsover.wordpress.com/2013/08/11/courage-in-decision-making-2/

[34]   Dr. Travis Bradberry: "How Successful People Overcome Uncertainty"
www.linkedin.com/pulse/how-successful-people-overcome-uncertainty-dr-travis-bradberry/

35   Beth Harper: "From Cowardly Lions To Courageous Decision Makers: What ClinOps Needs Now"
www.clinicalleader.com/doc/from-cowardly-lions-to-courageous-decision-makers-what-clinops-needs-now-0001

36   Pascal Fiedler: "Why your brand needs a signature story"
medium.com/the-mission/signaturestory-7bcec7faaedb

37   Going with your gut leads to more personal decisions
www.zmescience.com/science/news-science/gut-feeling-study-0432/

38   Onora O'Neill: "What we don't understand about trust"
www.ted.com/talks/onora_o_neill_what_we_don_t_understand_about_trust?language=en

39   *Hypothesis: An HPV Healing Experiment*
www.amazon.com/Teresa-Marie-Novak/e/B07CB8L61J

40   Ruth Chang: "How to make hard choices", Ted Talk
www.ted.com/talks/ruth_chang_how_to_make_hard_choices?language=en

41   Steven Johnson: "Decision-Making Should Be a Required Course in Every High School"
medium.com/s/story/farsighted-decision-making-should-be-a-required-course-in-every-high-school-6b5a836c1e1e

42   "Gratitude and well-being: A review and theoretical integration", Clinical Psychology Review
greatergood.berkeley.edu/pdfs/GratitudePDFs/2Wood-GratitudeWell-BeingReview.pdf

43   Fred McFeely Rogers, recipient of the Presidential Medal of freedom and a Peabody Award, Thank you at 10 minutes.
www.youtube.com/watch?v=907yEkALaAY

How to Cultivate Intuition

44   Emily Zulz: "Daniel Kahneman: Your Intuition Is Wrong, Unless These 3 Conditions Are Met"
www.thinkadvisor.com/2018/11/16/daniel-kahneman-do-not-trust-your-intuition-even-f/

45   Chris Cole: "A Smartphone App for Teaching Intuitive Diagnosis of Melanoma", Dr. Kolodney
www.physiciansweekly.com/a-smartphone-app-for-teaching-intuitive-diagnosis-of-melanoma/

46   Cardiac coherence breathing exercises, "Proper Breathing Brings Better Health", Scientific American
www.scientificamerican.com/article/proper-breathing-brings-better-health/?utm_medium=social&utm_content=organic&utm_source=twitter&utm_campaign=SciAm_&sf206620823=1

47   Rick Snyder: Everyone has 3 types of intuition. Here's how to use them to make better decisions."
www.fastcompany.com/90297993/everyone-has-3-types-of-intuition-heres-how-to-use-them-to-make-better-decisions

48   American Art Therapy Association: "Why adult coloring books are good for you"
www.cnn.com/2016/01/06/health/adult-coloring-books-popularity-mental-health/index.html

WHAT A DECISION COACH DOES AND DOESN'T DO

49   Linda Carroll: "Loved ones with health-care decision-making power often over-confident", Reuters
www.reuters.com/article/us-health-proxy/loved-ones-with-health-care-decision-making-power-often-over-confident-idUSKCN1NV2AF

50   Jonathan Kupersmith: "Decision Making: The Goal of Business Analysis"
www.b2ttraining.com/decision-making-the-goal-of-business-analysis/

HOW TO CREATE MOMENTS FOR KIDS TO EXPLORE CHOICE

51   Adapted from a piece originally published by Renee Jain on GoStrengths.com: "Help Your Kids Avoid the Indecision Blues"
www.huffpost.com/entry/help-your-kids-avoid-the-indecision-blues_b_4064633

52   Steven Johnson: "Decision-Making Should Be a Required Course in Every High School"
      medium.com/s/story/farsighted-decision-making-should-be-a-required-course-in-every-high-school-6b5a836c1e1e

53   Kate Rope, *Strong as a Mother: How to Stay Happy, Healthy and (Most Importantly) Sane From Pregnancy to Parenthood*, St. Martin's Griffin, 2018
      www.journalgazette.net/entertainment/20181004/guide-to-raising-good-decision-makers

54   "Bill Nye Explains the Scientific Method and His Greatest Accomplishment in Life"
      www.youtube.com/watch?v=_tcfyer6dho

Acknowledgements

55   My lifelong decision coaches.

www.ingramcontent.com/pod-product-compliance
Lightning Source LLC
Chambersburg PA
CBHW070934030426
42336CB00014BA/2664